HEADBUTLER.COM
THE 100 ESSENTIALS

BY JESSE KORNBLUTH

Books, music and movies
for people with more taste than time.

Also published by Head Butler Books:

"A Christmas Carol," by Charles Dickens, edited by Jesse Kornbluth
"The Greening of America," by Charles Reich

Cover and book design by Ines and Ena Talakic
www.inesandena.com

Head Butler icon design by Miles Hyman
www.MilesHyman.com

For the readers of HeadButler.com, who have trusted me enough to read books,
watch movies and listen to music that they might
never have otherwise encountered.

For my wife, who knows what to say, and when.

For our child, who insists she doesn't care.

TABLE OF CONTENTS

Introduction

I went to a school that required students to write a daily theme in English class.

The other kids hated that.

I was the only one who liked it.

Something else I liked is even more bizarre: When I was a too-smart-for-his-own-good teenager, one of my heroes was Pico della Mirandola (1463 – 1494), a Renaissance philosopher who, at 23, wrote 900 theses that, he said, held all human knowledge.

I thought that was extremely cool.

At some point, I thought I'd like to do what he did --- write 900 essays that sum up all I know and believe.

"At some point" did not mean "soon." I wrote books and magazine articles for decades. Then someone said, "You could be the Larry King of online." I considered Larry King's salary. I considered mine. Then I loaded the American Online software, logged on and never logged off. In 1997, AOL hired me to be its Editorial Director. As the most senior media veteran on staff, I got to interview the Dalai Lama, Eminem and many others. None of them said, "You know, you remind me of Larry King."

In 2002, I left AOL. From 2002 to 2004, I pretty much kept away from the Internet. Then my wife suggested something was missing in my life. As ever, she was right. So I started thinking about launching a site.

I knew I didn't want anything to do with a vast staff and a business model totally focused on revenue. Which left me with this: a one-man show. No one telling me what to do. No one asking me what to do. Just me, writing a daily theme. And why not, in the spirit of Pico della Mirandola, make it about my 900 favorite books, CDs and movies?

I did the math. Four reviews a week, fifty weeks a year; in 4 and 1/2 years, I could write about everything I loved. I imagined those 900 reviews would form a kind of "greatest hits" collection. And then I'd quit.

A decade after I launched HeadButler.com, I'm way beyond 900 reviews. And although there are no message boards, I seem to have created a vibrant community.

I know this because I get a lot of e-mail. Readers want help in choosing gifts. They want to find their next thrilling book, CD or movie. They want to know what's good for their kids. They want me to remind them about something I wrote about a few years ago. I'm happy to oblige, but these requests cut into my day.

For all of those readers --- and, I hope, many more --- here are my "100 essentials" in books, movies and music. The number is arbitrary; I started with a larger list. But the point of this book, like the idea behind HeadButler.com, is ruthless editing, or, as the online experts like to call it, "curation."

Some of these titles are recent releases; many aren't. One reason: Almost everything ever published, recorded or filmed is available on the Internet. Another reason is more flippant, but no less true: If it's new to you, it's new.

You'll see some "classics" here, but not because I want you to care about the kind of culture you were assigned in school --- for me, a classic is a bestseller that never stopped selling. There are no "political" books; there's more than enough politics elsewhere on the Web. There are oddball choices, like a book about Buddhism by a surfer and a memoir by a man who sells Birkin bags without, as Hermès does, making you wait as long as a year. There are glaring omissions --- no Rolling Stones, no Beatles --- and only one Dylan record, and the Dylan CD isn't one of his acknowledged masterpieces.

In "HeadButler.com: The 100 Essentials," I've created a book that can remind you of books, movies and music you loved but have forgotten about as well as books, movies and music you might enjoy. Because it's so subjective, it's also a book you can disagree with, maybe even want to argue with. Fine with me. My contact information is on the site --- www.headbutler.com --- which is where you might want to go soon and often.

--- Jesse Kornbluth
November, 2013

BOOKS

FICTION

Dorothy Baker: "Young Man with a Horn"

"What I'm going to do now is to write the story of Rick Martin's life, now that it's over, now that Rick is washed up and gone, as they say, to his rest."

That's the first line. You can guess what happens in these 192 pages.

At 20, Rick is bound for glory.

Before his 30th birthday, he's dead.

"Young Man With a Horn" is the fictionalized story of Leon Bismarck "Bix" Beiderbecke (1903 – 1931), who rocketed out of Davenport, Iowa with a sound so distinctive his only competition was Louis Armstrong. Bix was as shy as he was talented, damaged in a way that's still not quite clear. But he could play. Lord, could he play.

In a big band, Beiderbecke was the trumpet player with the spectacularly clear sound. As a pianist, he was an innovator. On both instruments, there's a combination of cool distance, hot jazz and the new kind of music coming from Europeans like Claude Debussy and Maurice Ravel. Louis Armstrong said it best: "Lots of cats tried to play like Bix; ain't none of them play like him yet."

No one could pin Bix down. An 8-measure solo here, a short phrase there --- he seemed to be making it up as he went along, but he couldn't be, no one was that inventive.

Dorothy Baker conjures all of it --- the life, the music, the recklessness, the shyness, the loneliness, the booze. She writes wonderful scenes:

-- the afternoon in a mission when young Rick Martin teaches himself Hymn 14 ("He stayed there until dark, and I can scarcely believe it myself, but the story goes that he could play the piano by dark; he could play number 14 on the piano by dark").

-- how he sits outside the Cotton Club night after night, in his early teens, listening to bands and memorizing their songs ("It wasn't that they were loud; it was that they were so firm about the way they played, no halfway measures, nothing fuzzy").

--- the night he gets to sit in with professionals ("Rick laid his cigarette in a groove above the keyboard where another cigarette had been laid sometime, sat down again, and said, 'What do you think of this?'").

--- how he gets hired to play in a band that caters to college kids in the California summer ("Rick dressed like a college boy, his hands were clean, and there was nothing much wrong with the way he talked, but there was something in his face that marked him as no college boy").

From there, it's the top of the mountain and down the hill.

Baker can see what's discordant in Rick Martin: "the gap between a man's musical ability and his ability to fit it to his own life."

She can editorialize: "He expected too much from music and he came to it with too much of a need."

She can nail a truth in the fewest possible words: A bandleader is "handsome in a way that doesn't mean anything."

And she knows the price of fame. Imagine a white lad in a world dominated by black artists who do it, he feels, just a bit better than he ever will. That's Bix Beiderbecke's relation to Louis Armstrong, and that's Rick Martin's sense of himself in comparison to his black idols. Is it surprising, then, that he never sleeps? That he drinks and drinks and drinks? That his romances are duds?

I first read this book when I was 12. I loved it because it did not condescend or sugarcoat. It took me inside the music --- it made me want to find an instrument and learn it. So I got myself a trumpet and tried to be Bix. Never made it. But then, no one ever has.

Got a kid who's into music? This is the book. Interested in the Jazz Age? Ditto. Or just looking for a short novel that you can't put down? Here you go. ∎

James Cain: "Mildred Pierce"

James Cain is no longer a name to conjure with. Sad. He was the master of chilly, sexy fiction that raised the hair on the back of the neck of the censors. Of the '30s and '40s crime novelists, no one --- not Raymond Chandler, not Dashiell Hammett --- could jam as much nastiness into so few pages.

Two books made him immortal. His first novel, published in 1934, was "The Postman Always Rings Twice," 128 very efficient pages filled with sex, violence and some unforgettably nasty people. And two years later, "Double Indemnity," 115 very efficient pages filled with sex, violence and some unforgettably nasty people.

"Mildred Pierce," published in 1941, is a very different kind of book. Though hardly padded, it's twice as long as Cain's first novels. There's a murder, but its real violence is verbal and psychological. And because it begins in 1931 and ends in 1940, you can't ignore a fact that overhangs everything in the novel: the Great Depression.

What's the story about?

A man tends to his lawn, showers, gets dressed, tells his wife that he's going for a walk. She knows better --- he's going to see his mistress "and then unbutton that red dress she's always wearing without any brassieres under it." But it's not the mistress that annoys his wife most. It's the way he's without work and not exactly looking for any.

Now the author steps in, and I, for one, marvel at how Cain is both concise and vivid: "They spoke quickly, as though they were saying things that scalded their mouths, and had to be cooled with spit."

Because the characters don't just plot and scheme in the dark, I see "Mildred Pierce" as Cain's best novel. Here the shapely, sexy woman is a wife and mother who wants to stay married. She throws her husband out as a statement of self-respect. It's a costly gesture. As a friend says, "You've joined the biggest army on earth. You're the great American institution that never gets mentioned on Fourth of July --- a grass widow with two small children to support. The dirty bastards."

Mildred's assets are few. She can bake. And she's got a bod for sin. "Her brassiere ballooned a little, with an extremely seductive burden." Although she's got great gams, she feels she's slightly bow-legged, so she takes short steps when she walks. To great effect --- "her bottom twitched in a wholly provocative way."

It's not long before two realities collide. She has no trouble finding a lover (and discovering that she enjoys sex) --- but it's impossible to get a job. For one thing, she is without qualifications. For another, she fears that her eldest daughter, the beautiful and haughty Veda, will scorn her if she wears a waitress's uniform or becomes a clerk in a store.

But a waitress she becomes. And money flows in. Veda is, as expected, horrified. She says Mildred has "degraded" the family. Mildred's response: She spanks Veda silly. To no point. Veda crawls to a couch, laughs and whispers: "A waitress."

It is then that Mildred realizes that she fears her daughter's judgment, "her snobbery, her contempt, her unbreakable spirit." She resolves to open a restaurant, to be a waitress no more. And she thanks her daughter for prodding her to aim higher: "We'll have something. And it'll all be on account of you. Every good thing that happens is on account of you, if Mother only had the good sense to know it."

On the eve of the opening of Mildred's restaurant, she spends the weekend with a society swell and becomes his lover. Back home, her younger daughter has spiked a fever and is in the hospital. The death scene is terrible. Even worse is Mildred's reaction: *Thank God it wasn't Veda.*

You think your kids have foul, disrespectful mouths? Listen to Veda: "With this money I can get away from you. From you and your chickens and your pies and your kitchens and everything that smells of grease. I can get away from this shack with its cheap furniture. And this town and its dollar days, and its women that wear uniforms and its men that wear overalls."

Through it all, Mildred is Mother Courage. Her will and her work ethic dazzle. But can Veda be redeemed?

Most parents have, at one time or another, a child whose ingratitude is sharper than a serpent's tooth.

Well, here's the worst case --- read it and weep for Mildred, then count your blessings. ■

"The Stories of John Cheever"

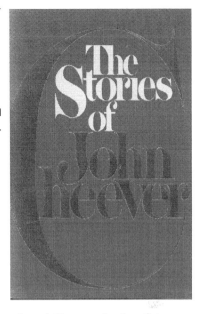

In 1979, when I interviewed Cheever for The New York Times Magazine, he was a youthful, wiry 67.

We recently marked what would have been his hundredth birthday.

Of the many profiles I've written, why is my Cheever piece still so vivid for me? The answer has less to do with the man than with his work. That summer, I'd rented a cheap house in Southampton. In the mornings, I sat in the yard and read Cheever. In the afternoons, I read him on the beach. It took a week to polish off the 700 pages of his stories.

I followed that delicious, once-in-a-lifetime experience with an afternoon at Cheever's house in Westchester. He liked to bicycle each morning, so we saddled up and rode around his neighborhood ("Peter Frampton lives there"), and then, over iced tea, we sat and talked on the porch.

Cheever gave good interview ("What did I learn from Ernest Hemingway? Not to put a shotgun in my mouth"). Not surprising; some writers are great talkers. Cheever had another reason to be extravagantly quotable --- he was afraid I'd learn that he was bi-sexual and include that in my piece. In 1979, that would have been a career-ender for a literary titan of Cheever's generation.

Cheever need not have worried. I suspected nothing and heard no gossip --- I was too busy being dazzled by his stories. "The American Chekhov," the shorthand had it. Yes, in the sense that Cheever, like Chekhov, could take even the smallest moment and turn it into material. But that description seemed unhelpful, because Cheever was so completely American --- so completely New England, really.

Cheever wrote many of these stories in the storage room of his New York apartment. In the morning, he'd dress as if he were going to an office, but he rode the elevator down to the basement, where he'd hang up his suit pants and start writing. Some days he'd get all the way to the end of a story; every night, he'd kill a bottle of liquor. Ah, the 1950s....

There are Cheever stories you've probably read in school: "The Swimmer" and "The

Enormous Radio." There are stories --- like "The Hartleys" --- that you wouldn't have loved when you were younger but are oh-so-meaningful now. And there are stories that will make you feel as if you're reading about the characters in "Mad Men."

If you want to audition Cheever, seek out the first story in the book: "Goodbye, My Brother." It's about a WASP family with one of those big houses on the bluffs of Nantucket. The family's three grown sons, a daughter, a mother, various spouses and kids have assembled for a late-summer vacation. Swimming, drinking, family dinners, club dances, game nights at home: This reunion should look like a Ralph Lauren commercial. Why it doesn't: Lawrence --- the youngest brother, the one who "looks like a Puritan cleric" --- has arrived.

We all know people like Lawrence, people who try "to spoil every pleasure." We endure them because we don't see much of them. But to share a house with Lawrence, to have your two weeks of vacation darkened by his omnipresent scowl --- it drives the narrator, an otherwise mild-mannered high school teacher, to spill the blood of his blood.

Lawrence departs in a huff on a gorgeous late-summer morning --- not that, from the ferry, he'd see its beauty. And the narrator? The ending of his relationship with his brother is inspiration for a final look at much more than a family drama. Here's the last paragraph:

Oh, what can you do with a man like that? What can you do? How can you dissuade his eyes in a crowd from seeking out the cheek with acne, the infirm hand; how can you teach him to respond to the inestimable greatness of the race, the harsh surface beauty of life; how can you put his finger for him on the obdurate truths before which fear and horror are powerless? The sea that morning was iridescent and dark. My wife and my sister were swimming -- Diana and Helen -- and I saw their uncovered heads, black and gold in the dark water. I saw them come out and I saw that they were naked, unshy, beautiful and full of grace, and I watched the naked women walk out of the sea.

I ask you: Is not that one of the most beautiful pieces of writing you've ever read? ■

Maurice Dekobra:
"The Madonna of the Sleeping Cars"

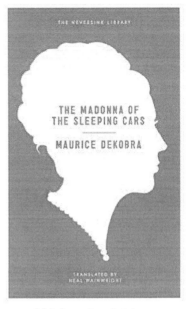

Maurice Dekobra's name is now almost completely forgotten, but in 1927 he published a novel called "The Madonna of the Sleeping Cars" that sold a million copies in France.

In 1928, The New York Times described him as "the biggest seller of any living French writer --- or dead one either." Fifteen of his novels became films. ("Madonna" was filmed twice.) Over his career, he sold 15 million books in 32 languages, and his kind of writing --- a slick blend of journalism and high-society intrigue --- acquired a brand name: dekobrisme.

"The Madonna of the Sleeping Cars" went out of print in 1948.

It's finally back. So let me introduce you.

Maurice Dekobra (1885-1973) began his career as a translator (Daniel Defoe, Jack London, Mark Twain). In the early 1920s, he was a journalist and foreign correspondent. His fiction reflects his training --- it's grounded in the news, is briskly paced and has an unusually tart point-of-view.

The plot, as these things go, is simple. Lady Diana Wynham is a London widow known for her beauty ("the type of woman who would have brought tears to the eyes of John Ruskin"). She is just as well known for her unabashed amorality. Presented with a list of her lovers, in chronological order, she has only one correction: "Excuse me, but they were contemporaneous."

Lady Diana is about to be ruined financially. Her sole hope of salvation is 10,000 acres of Russian oil land that her late husband, the English ambassador to the court of St. Petersburg, received as a gift from the government of Nicholas II. It is --- in 1920s money --- worth 50 million dollars.

The bad news: Russia's Bolshevist government has confiscated all foreign property.

The good news: Leonid Varichkine will get it back for Lady Diana in exchange for "one night" of love.

What are a few illicit hours to a woman "who could never be happy without a great deal of money?" But Lady Diana is as clever as she is amoral. She proposes a better deal.

"Madonna" starts in London, makes stops in Berlin, an Arabian prison and a yacht in the Mediterranean, with a melodramatic climax in a castle in Scotland. In addition to distance, lessons are learned: a Communist can be converted to capitalism for less money than you might think, and "passing infractions of fidelity" are "trivial."

I've dipped into a few other Dekobras. They're not awful. But "Madonna" is clearly his showpiece. It's a fun, terse story that is as convincing about London drawing rooms as it is about Russian execution chambers. And you care about Lady D. ■

GUY DE MAUPASSANT: "BEL-AMI"

George --- the kind of handsome guy from the country who, for lack of a better thing to do, joins the Army --- finishes his military service without a prospect in the world. He moves to the big city, because that's where opportunity lies.

He gets a lousy job and is totally frustrated. One evening he runs into Charles, an old Army buddy who's now a newspaper editor. Charles has an idea: George should write up his wartime experiences, Charles will publish them, and then George will have some business and social credibility.

One problem: George can't write.

No problem: Charles's wife will help him.

She does. A job follows. And social invitations. And rich lovers. And thus begins George's rise to the top. We've read this story before, haven't we? More often than not, the main character is a woman; her beauty is her calling card, and then her wit and charm do the rest. A man who uses women is a nice twist on an old story.

Indeed, it's the story of "Bel-Ami," the novel that was Guy de Maupassant's masterpiece. Publication date: 1885.

If you think of de Maupassant at all, it's as a short-story writer. Somewhere in your education, you read "The Necklace" and decided that de Maupassant was something like O.Henry. Fair enough --- de Maupassant did write some 300 short stories, and many of them end with a wry twist. But de Maupassant was so much more than that.

For one thing, Gustave Flaubert was his mentor; for readers who have savored the flawless storytelling in "Madame Bovary," that says a lot. Through Flaubert, he met Zola, Turgenev and Henry James. And unlike George Duroy, the main character of "Bel-Ami," de Maupassant had no difficulty getting published, making money --- or finding amusing women.

In the 1870s, de Maupassant contracted syphilis; by the 1880s, as he was writing

"Bel-Ami," he knew he was doomed. So he poured everything into the book --- from a bitingly realistic philosophy of life to some of the hottest romantic scenes in 19th century fiction. Then he tried to kill himself by cutting his throat. He was put in a mental hospital and died the following year --- at age 43.

The glory of "Bel-Ami" (French for "good friend") is the plot. Though you will probably detest George and his methods --- think of a super-slick George Hamilton --- the story moves so fast and the writing is so clean and the smut is just so evocative that you hurtle on despite yourself. There's a dinner party in a Paris restaurant, where good wine and fine food and some ribald suggestions from George enflame the two couples, and then there's a carriage ride back to the home of George's married dinner companion...

But it is not that George is a predator and the women are easy prey. In Paris in the 1870s and 1880s, many are married and bored; they know what they're doing. A few women are virtuous; George ruins them. And then there is Madeleine, the wife of his friend the newspaper editor. She's smart and cool and modern as Prada. Listen to her:

Marriage, to me, is not a chain but an association. I must be free, entirely unfettered, in all my actions, my coming and my going; I can tolerate neither control, jealousy nor criticism as to my conduct. I pledge my word, however, never to compromise the name of the man I marry, nor to render him ridiculous in the eyes of the world. But that man must promise to look upon me as an equal, an ally, and not as an inferior, or as an obedient, submissive wife. My ideas, I know, are not like those of other people, but I shall never change them.

She sees through George --- or does she? I don't want to spoil the story, but you'll think quite a lot about a choice she makes late in the book. And about George's visit to his parents. And an amazing painting that's unveiled at a rich man's party. About mothers and daughters, and this guy's eagerness to seduce them both. About --- but there's no end to it. "Bel-Ami" is just one of those books that's hard to put down. The faster he rises, the worse he behaves; you can't wait to see how George will be punished for his crimes against women.

And then you get to the ending. Suddenly you have to consider the morality of these characters --- and your own --- all over again. How annoying! But totally worth it, for "Bel-Ami" is a novel you will read again and again, a novel you'll press on your friends, a novel you can argue with for years. ∎

Alan Furst:
"Mission to Paris"

If you have a deadline looming or even a busy week, the absolute last thing you want to do is crack open "Mission to Paris" and think you're going to read just a chapter, because you're not.

You're going to read when you shouldn't be reading. You'll read at lunch. On the street. Deep into the night.

But if you then try to convey your enthusiasm for "Mission to Paris" to someone who has never read any of Alan Furst's 13 novels, you may have a hard time. These are spy thrillers by category, but in this book, the hero is a Hollywood movie star who, in 1938, is "loaned out" to a Parisian producer to play the lead in a French film. In total violation of convention, there's a romance with a woman who's not a swimsuit model. As for suspense, even before you start a Furst novel set in Europe during the run-up to World War II, you know at least part of the ending — the hero is not going to kill Hitler and save the world.

So why are Alan Furst's novels so addictive?

Just read the first paragraph of "Mission to Paris."

In Paris, the evenings of September are sometimes warm, excessively gentle, and, in the magic particular to that city, irresistibly seductive. The autumn of 1938 began in just such weather and on the terraces of the best cafés, in the famous restaurants, at the dinner parties one wished to attend, the conversation was, of necessity, lively and smart: fashion, cinema, love affairs, politics, and, yes, the possibility of war—that too had its moment. Almost anything, really, except money. Or, rather, German money. A curious silence, for hundreds of millions of francs — tens of millions of dollars — had been paid to some of the most distinguished citizens of France since Hitler's ascent to power in 1933. But maybe not so curious, because those who had taken the money were aware of a certain shadow in these transactions and, in that shadow, the people who require darkness for the kind of work they do.

An immense amount of information is conveyed in those 155 words.

The tension between the lively start of the fall season in Paris and the conversation no one wants to have about German money. The way that money compromises the rich Frenchmen who take it. The presence of shady characters. And, not least, the feeling you get when you have fallen under the spell of a master storyteller.

And that's just the first paragraph.

The first chapter follows a French fool who absconds with enough of that German money to live comfortably in another country for years. Think he gets away? Or do you think we see, in brisk, no nonsense prose, the efficiency of the German operation in France — in 1938?

All of that suggests what awaits Fredric Stahl when he arrives in Paris to make a movie. He's no matinee idol: "He couldn't punch another man, he wasn't Clark Gable, and he couldn't fight a duel, he was not Errol Flynn. But neither was he Charles Boyer — he wasn't so *sophisticated*. Mostly he played a warm man in a cold world."

The Germans, knowing Stahl was born in Vienna, are interested in him. And they want so little: come to Berlin, just to judge a festival of films about mountains. $10,000 for a day's work. Lufthansa will fly him over and back.

Stahl is less than interested. But then he gets a taste of German commitment to the triumph of the Reich. (As Goebbels's people liked to say, "We don't send out press releases. We send out operatives, and then *other* people send out press releases.")

Stahl prudently consults an American spymaster.

"You're not a spy," the officer tells him. "That takes nerves of steel, and soon enough becomes a full-time job." A "but" follows: "If, in your time here you, ah, *stumble* on something, something important, it wouldn't be a bad idea if you let me know about it."

And that happens.

Furst's main characters are drawn into espionage by circumstance. Then they see there are good guys and bad guys, and at some point, you've got to decide where you stand. So although these novels are about Europe in the years before World War II, they're also exquisite little morality plays about right now, right here.

But mostly, damned if they don't make you think, "I've got to get to Paris, and soon." ∎

John Green:
"The Fault in Our Stars"

Sometimes you read a book and it fills you with this weird evangelic zeal, and you become convinced that the shattered world will never be put back together unless and until all living humans read the book.

Hazel Lancaster says that in "The Fault in Our Stars," a novel that leaps off the page and makes you think of those books in your life, and more --- that this book knows you so well it reads you. That's a pretty neat trick.

But that's not John Green's best trick. That one is astonishing: Days after I finished reading his book, I was still shaking. Family and friends will confirm that "The Fault in Our Stars" was all I could talk about. I hated that I'd read it because there was nothing I wanted to do more than read it again for the first time.

Two facts make this a very unlikely obsession:

1) This is a Young Adult (YA) novel --- a book for teenagers.

2) Both main characters are teenagers who have cancer.

But it's not like this is some kind of cheesy teenage "Love Story."

It's more like "The Fault in Our Stars" is the best novel --- the smartest, most clever, most emotional-but-not-exploitive adult novel --- you've read in a long, long time, but somehow kids found out about it first and claimed it as their own. Which they have done, big time, and in astonishing numbers. "The Fault in Our Stars" opened on the New York Times list for Children's Chapter Books at #1 and stayed there for five weeks. Three months after "The Fault in Our Stars" was published, NPR did a survey of the best YA novels... ever. "The Fault in Our Stars" came in at #4. And, at the end of 2012, TIME named it the best novel of the year. Not the best YA novel. The best novel. Period.

Why the love?

Simple as this: John Green doesn't write teenagers. He writes smart, funny, verbal, real people who happen to find themselves in young bodies. This is fortunate, because the young --- the best of them, anyway --- are brimming over with Thoughts and Ideals and Questions. They... just... care. Deeply. As we used to care before we grew up and found ourselves playing games that had more to do with Success and Money than Truth and Eternity.

Yeah, but this is "a cancer book."

No. It isn't. Hazel, the 16-year-old narrator, is very clear about that, and she ought to know. When she was 13, she almost died, and there was that grim scene in the ICU when the cancer was joined by pneumonia and her mother asked "Are you ready?" and she said she was and her dad was trying not to sob and then --- surprise, surprise --- her cancer doctor managed to drain her lungs and she got admitted to a trial for a drug that didn't work 70% of the time but it worked in her, and now she's 16 and going to Wednesday night Support Group meetings.

Is Hazel going to tell you a story that becomes a cancer book?

No way.

"Cancer books suck," she says. "Like, in cancer books, the cancer person starts a charity that raises money to fight cancer, right? And this commitment to charity reminds the cancer person of the essential goodness of humanity and makes him/her feel loved and encouraged because s/he will leave a cancer-curing legacy."

Hazel knows better. That's because she has a favorite book --- the book she's an evangelist for --- called "An Imperial Affliction," and in that book, the main character "decides that being a person with cancer who starts a cancer charity is a bit narcissistic, so she starts a charity called The Anna Foundation for People with Cancer Who Want to Cure Cholera." A bad joke, but you get the idea: "Cancer is a side effect of the process of dying, as is almost everything, really."

That attitude makes Hazel an unlikely candidate for romance, but one Wednesday at Support Group she meets Augustus Waters, who is 17 and shockingly handsome. He had "a little touch of osteosarcoma a year and a half ago," and half of one leg had to be amputated, but he's fine now. The only reason he's come to the meeting is to support a friend who will, in a month, have both eyes removed.

Augustus isn't put off by the tubes in Hazel's nose or the oxygen tank she drags around with her. To him, she's "a millennial Natalie Portman. Like 'V for Vendetta' Natalie Portman." To her, he's "a tenured professor in the Department of Slightly Crooked Smiles with a dual appointment in the Department of Having a Voice That Made My Skin Feel Like Skin."

Love, in short. But it doesn't come easily and it doesn't happen fast. There is considerable uncertainty, in fact, given his romantic past and her terminal condition. So they talk about Magritte, Zeno's tortoise paradox, Maslow's Hierarchy of Needs.

They make jokes about their friends in the world of the professionally ill: "I've gotten really hot since you went blind." They share odd facts: There are about 98 billion dead people.

At last they open to one another. Their romance is epic, and then some, and they're not ashamed to cop to it. And, along the way, they slip in terrific little truths, lines that make you reach for a pen: "You don't get to choose if you get hurt in this world, but you do have some say in who hurts you."

You'll notice that I'm not saying much about what happens in this novel. A lot does, and you don't see it coming --- there is a surprise every few pages. And then you get to page 313, and it's over. How did that happen? How did you smile so much? How did you cry so hard and yet feel cleansed and triumphant at the end? And if John Green is so good, why does he write YA novels?

It's not a cancer book. Cancer books suck. This book does everything but. ■

Denis Johnson:
"Jesus' Son"

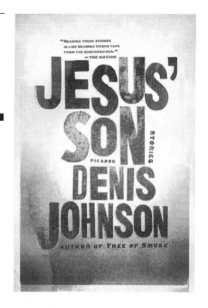

A guy has a knife stuck in his eye; a drugged-out hospital orderly saves him without quite knowing what he's done.

Another guy gets shot in a farmhouse, for no reason.

A third guy overdoses.

Prison looms for everyone.

And it all takes place in the gloomy flatland of the Midwest, circa 1971.

"Jesus' Son" is one of the ten funniest books I've ever read.

You sputter: This is a bummer. Indeed it is. And if you think heroin addiction is tawdry (and it is, it is) and the people who use hard drugs are losers (and they are, they are) and there is Nothing Funny about an overdose, then these eleven stories are so not for you.

But if you have a taste for Black Humor or an appreciation of outlandish characters --- or even an ear for brilliant writing --- this 160-page book will give you the most delightful two-to-three hours of reading you've experienced in a long, long time. Well, maybe not three hours. Maybe a lot more --- for if, like me, you occasionally find yourself in need of the kind of laugh that only a book can provide, your eye goes instinctively to "Jesus' Son." Your hand involuntarily removes it from the shelf. And before you know it, you're lost in the world of this remarkable book.

Let's just consider the first story, "Car Crash While Hitchhiking." It is exactly that. The narrator is a hitchhiker who, on one leg of his trip that day, has been fed pills by a salesman. He is now wired and omniscient:

I knew every raindrop by its name. I sensed everything before it happened. I knew a certain Oldsmobile would stop for me even before it slowed, and by the sweet voices of the family inside that we'd have an accident in the storm.

The accident occurs. The driver dies. His wife survives. Now we're at the hospital:

Down the hall came the wife. She was glorious, burning. She didn't know yet that her husband was dead. We knew. That's what gave her such power over us. The doctor took her into a room with a desk at the end of the hall, and from under the closed door a slab of brilliance radiated as if, by some stupendous process, diamonds were being incinerated in there. What a pair of lungs! She shrieked as I imagined an eagle would shriek. It felt wonderful to be alive to hear it! I've gone looking for that feeling everywhere.

And then comes an ending that confounds all expectation:

It was raining. Gigantic ferns leaned over us. The forest drifted down a hill. I could hear a creek rushing down rocks. And you, you ridiculous people, you expect me to help you.

That last line --- directly addressed to the reader --- announces that these will not be "traditional" stories, with characters that describe their troubles and fix them. This is a world of the lost: freaks abandoned by God, people who connect with holiness only (in the words of the Lou Reed song that provides the title) "when I'm rushing on my run."

The power of these stories is the writing, first and foremost, but there is also the sense that these stories are real. As Johnson recalls, "I was addicted to everything.... When I was 21, I went into my first psych ward for alcohol." Then he moved on to drugs. "But I was not a constant junkie. You can't just go into a drugstore and say, 'I'll have some heroin, please.' You have to be prepared to enter into all kinds of adventures that I wasn't strong enough for."

Those adventures included study at the University of Iowa with Raymond Carver. He wrote "Jesus' Son" because he owed the IRS $10,000 and had these stories in his head:

I never even wrote that book, I just wrote it down. I would tell these stories apropos of nothing about when I was drinking and using and people would say, "You should write these things down." I was probably 35 when I wrote the first story. The voice is kind of a mix in that it has a young voice, but it's also someone who's looking back. I like that kind of double vision. So I worked on them once in a while, then I started using stories I heard other people tell, and then I started making some up. Pretty soon it was fiction. Then I just forgot about it. I thought, I'm not going to parade my defects, my history of being a spiritual cripple, out in front of a lot of other people. But once in a while I'd write a little more --- I would just hear the voices.

He's written many more books and won awards, but "Jesus' Son" is the one that readers cherish. Is it that there's something about hair-raising stories told by addicts that we just can't resist? Or is it just the voices? Either way, these stories are... addictive.■

John Le Carré:
The Spy Who Came in from the Cold"

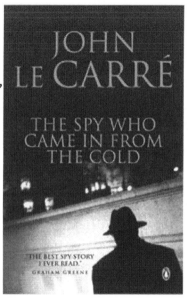

In 1963, David Cornwell published his third novel. Because he was then an agent for British Intelligence, he used, as his government required, a pseudonym: "John Le Carré."

Graham Greene, who pretty much invented the modern spy novel, called "The Spy Who Came in from the Cold" "the best spy story I ever read." He understood immediately that, in a decade when James Bond was all the rage, "Spy" revolutionized the spy novel. The Bond books --- and, even more, the Bond movies --- were thrill rides. The suave hero never mussed his tux. He had no need to; his car had more armament than one of Patton's brigades. The explosions that went off just a few feet from him always were just background flash. And, of course, he possessed the ultimate weapon --- his deadly quips, capable of killing any villain within earshot.

For Le Carré, spycraft was the antithesis of a glamour profession. It was thinking and planning, waiting and watching, and lying --- always lying. It operated by a single moral law: results. You may be assured that good people were betrayed along the way.

"Spy" was an instant classic precisely because Le Carré showed readers exactly what Intelligence is about --- sometimes a roll of film, more often a list of names, never an atom bomb in a briefcase. Even better, it revealed how the trick is done. And, most of all, it asked a question: Us and Them --- how different are we, really?

In London, men schemed long and hard to think up ways to misdirect the Communists. In East Berlin, men much like them plotted to deceive and damage the Brits. Between them was the Wall — and a brightly lit, barb wired checkpoint.

The Wall is where this novel starts. Alec Leamas, a 50-year-old British agent, waits at the West Berlin checkpoint for a German --- a British agent --- who's in danger of being found out. Tonight, he's crossing over. You get the scene quickly: coffee, cigarettes, idle chatter. And then you see the man on a bicycle. He stops at the East Berlin gate, shows his papers, pedals on. But then he hears something. He pedals faster. Shots are fired. He sags, falls. Leamas, the ultimate realist, "hoped to God he was dead."

The career of Alec Leamas certainly is; he failed to get his man across. And this leads to an opportunity for his employers. They would love to discredit --- or, better, destroy --- Mundt, head of German Intelligence in East Berlin. The way they'll do this? Retire Leamas. Watch him sink into booze and despair. Let him be recruited by the East Germans. And then, in his debriefings, let him present these Communists with evidence that Mundt has been taking money from the Brits — that Mundt is a British agent.

This is mental chess. It calls for 24/7 acting skills. And the bar is set high. Leamas, flawlessly failing. Leamas, jailed. Leamas, released and bitter. Lemeas, expertly recruited by the Germans. Leamas, credibly sneering at his new employers. But that's only technique. Idealism? Patriotism? Good luck finding any.

Let me interrupt to tell you something important about the author. His mother left home when he was 5 years old; he didn't see her again until he was 21. His father was "a confidence trickster and a jailbird." Le Carré has said: "I was a spy before they ever recruited me. If you are brought up to believe that your home is an extremely dangerous place...."

In his writing, he says, 'I always try to identify with one character in a book and appoint him my secret sharer." Here, that character is Alec Leamas. But there is also a father: Control, the head of MI5.

I'm not going to spoil the book for you, but I do ask you to read with one thought in the back of your head: For this writer, what does a father do? ∎

Somerset Maugham: "Cakes and Ale"

His parents were known as "Beauty and the Beast." Once someone asked the lovely Mrs. Maugham how she remained faithful to her ugly little husband. "He never hurts my feelings," she said.

She was equally tender to her youngest son, William. When he was just eight years old, she died.

Seventy years later, William Somerset Maugham was still saying, "I shall never get over her death. I shall never get over it."

Two years later, his father died.

Willie Maugham, who had lived so long in Paris that he spoke no English, was shipped back to relatives in the English countryside. He had a clubfoot. And a stammer. He wanted to be a writer; he was persuaded to go to medical school. When he was 23, he produced a novel. It was a huge success. Medicine was forgotten.

By 1930, when "Cakes and Ale" hit the bookstores, Maugham had published "Of Human Bondage" and "The Moon and Sixpence" and a book of innovative spy stories. He was the highest-paid, most famous writer in the world. No mystery why --- his books were chatty and easy to read. They went down smooth and whole, like oysters. Once consumed, they presented no bulk. This was deliberate; Maugham had gone to school on de Maupassant and Chekhov, practiced writing stories that had no adjectives and, with considerable sweat, forged a prose style that read like conversation.

Maugham was not known as a bomb-thrower, but "Cakes and Ale" in 1930 changed that. The novel was a scandal. Not for the sex. For literary reasons — it starts with a vicious portrait of "Roy Kear," a popular writer of second-rate novels clearly modeled on a then-noted English writer. The odd thing: Kear is important only for getting the story started, he couldn't be a more minor character.

Kear, in any event, gets things going by leaving a message for Willie Ashenden, now a moderately successful, extremely observant writer. Good manners require Ashenden to accept an invitation for lunch.

There, to his surprise, Kear turns the conversation to Edward Driffield, the venerable English novelist (Maugham modeled him on Thomas Hardy) who wrote so many deadly boring books over so many decades that he is regarded as a master.

It turns out that, as a boy of 15, Ashenden was befriended by Edward Driffield and his first wife, Rosie. Roy Kear is writing an adoring biography of Driffield; he'd love Ashenden to share those memories. Instead, Ashenden drifts down memory lane and tells us the story no one knows --- the truth about the Driffield marriage.

Ashenden's memories seem to be a chronicle of small-town snobbery. In the countryside where young Ashenden (and Maugham) spends school vacations, the Driffields are not respectable. Edward is a writer, thus automatically suspect. And Rosie --- well, she has a past. Young Ashenden is aware of their checkered reputation, but he is hungrier for adult friendship than he is for social propriety. The Driffields become his second family --- until they suddenly bolt, leaving debts and questions behind them.

Years pass. Ashenden is now a medical student in London. He runs into Rosie; their friendship resumes. But Ashenden is twenty --- old enough to grasp, however dimly, that although Rosie seems to love her husband, she is repeatedly unfaithful to him. Soon enough, he becomes her lover. One of them, anyway, for Ashenden must confront an idea that few men can handle: women's right to sexual freedom.

Roy Kear can't. Here he is, pumping Willie Ashenden:

"I suppose she was awful."
"I don't recollect that."
"She must have been dreadfully common. She was a barmaid, wasn't she?"
"Yes."
"I wonder why the devil he married her. I've always been given to understand that she was extremely unfaithful to him."
"Extremely."
"Do you remember at all what she was like?"
"Yes, very distinctly," I smiled. "She was sweet."

Not what Kear wants to hear. Much later Ashenden spells it out for him:

"She was a very simple woman. Her instincts were healthy and ingenuous. She loved to make people happy. She loved love."
"Do you call that love?"
"Well, then, the act of love. She was naturally affectionate. When she liked anyone, it was quite natural for her to go to bed with him. She never thought twice about it. It was not vice; it wasn't lasciviousness; it was her nature. She gave herself as naturally as the sun gives heat or the flowers their perfume. It was a pleasure to her and she liked to give

pleasure to others. It was a pleasure to her and she liked to give pleasure to others. It had no effect on her character; she remained sincere, unspoiled, and artless."

Whew! That's a long way from bike rides in the country, even further from lunch with Roy Kear in a London club. And although "Cakes and Ale" is a relatively short novel — it's a crisp 300 pages — there are many more twists in it. I won't spoil them for you.

It's been fashionable for decades to dismiss Maugham as a mere storyteller, as if the ability to tell stories is a second-rate gift. But unless you are a snootball critic, stories are what you read fiction for. In "Cakes and Ale," Maugham juggles half a dozen characters without breaking a sweat. The novel seems formless and weightless, a tale told by a friend over drinks. You cannot imagine how hard it is to do this.

Of all his books, Maugham considered "Cakes and Ale" his favorite. Read it and you'll see why.■

ALICE MUNRO: "DEAR LIFE"

I did not go home for my mother's last illness or for her funeral. I had two small children and nobody in Vancouver to leave them with. We could barely have afforded the trip, and my husband had a contempt for formal behavior, but why blame it on him? I felt the same. We say of some things that they can't be forgiven, or that we will never forgive ourselves. But we do --- we do it all the time.

These are the final words in "Dear Life," a book of short stories from Nobel Prize winner Alice Munro. Because she is now 81, it is possibly her last. I wish I could judge this book against her 14 other collections of stories, but the truth is, I've never read her until now, and I wouldn't have read these 13 stories unless I'd read some raves and read snippets and realized --- yet again --- that I've been a damn fool all these years.

Cynthia Ozick has said of Munro: "She is our Chekhov and is going to outlast most of her contemporaries."

That's high-toned praise, just so you know how respected Munro is. And then there are the prizes. Who knew literature had so many?

But who reads for "literary" reasons?

Not me. I read --- especially fiction --- because I want to know how it feels to be someone else. To think like someone else. To have someone else's adventures, crises, romances and triumphs. Because, for an hour or a day, I want out of my life.

When I love a book, I like to say that I started reading and didn't stop until I was done. Not with these stories. You can't. One a day is a full meal, and then you have to go away and process it. Because these aren't really stories --- they're compressed novels, entire lives told in 30 pages. Others writers do something like this, but I can't think of another who does it within the apparent frame of a traditionally told story.

For example, the first story begins like this: "Once Peter had brought her suitcase on board the train he seemed eager to get himself out of the way." Peter, we learn, is

Greta's husband --- and this is the last we'll see of him. This is a woman's story, the story of a young poet, traveling with her daughter. Something happens on that train, and it's sexy and scary and not anything you expect --- and then, at the end, something else happens, something you thought was not at all likely. It happens fast, and it hits you hard, and there's no way you rush on to the next.

The next story also starts with a train trip. With good reason: Munro is Canadian. She married young to escape her father's failing mink farm and her mother's Parkinson's, and she had children, and she wrote and wrote, pushing her kids away when they interrupted her. All this took place a long time ago, when small town life was a world and women who broke the rules were notorious in that world. Naturally Munro would be drawn to characters that have a dream, who want more, who have no roadmap or mentors and have to figure it out themselves. As she writes: "It would become hard to explain, later on in her life, just what was okay in that time and what was not."

A young woman goes to teach in a remote sanitarium --- so remote she describes the sky as an "immense enchantment." She trades one small world for another. Romance with the doctor? You can see it coming. What happens after? Pure surprise. Two sisters, a gravel pit filled with water. A daughter of liberals spending a year with her hard-ass uncle. An unmarried woman, having an affair and dealing with blackmail. A woman needs to get a prescription filled. An elderly couple discusses a joint suicide --- and then his old lover shows up.

There's a story about a policeman with a sick wife. He devotes himself to her, even moves to the city so she can get better care. At last she dies. And he has to walk out of the hospital: "He'd thought that it had happened long before with Isabel, but it hadn't. Not until now. She had existed and now she did not... And before long, he found himself outside, pretending that he had as ordinary and good a reason as anybody else to put one foot ahead of the other."

The lives of little people. We see them on the street, and, if we are curious, we wonder about their lives. Alice Munro does our homework for us --- she inhabits those lives. Her judgments are sure. And tough. And also... human.

Like the words at the end of the book. They are from an autobiographical sketch, her first, and, she says, her last.

We say of some things that they can't be forgiven, or that we will never forgive ourselves. But we do --- we do it all the time.

Ain't it the truth? ∎

TIM O'BRIEN: "THE THINGS THEY CARRIED"

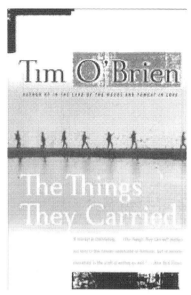

I went to the Costa Rican rain forest. That climate is much like Vietnam, so I took along the paperback of "The Things They Carried." One afternoon, when the temperature was 95 and so was the humidity, I sat down with this collection of short stories. Two hours and 271 pages later, I got up.

What's so great? The people. O'Brien delivers a company of American soldiers during the Vietnam war with unsentimental tenderness: the guy who will get his head blown off seconds after smoking a joint, the guy who will commit suicide years after the war, the guy who will die in the muck, the guys who will find him --- and the Vietnamese soldier O'Brien kills. There is no larger war, no deeper significance. Life has been reduced to a jungle and these men.

If we were talking about fiction, we would say something like: 'The voice of the narrator is strong and authentic.' But this is something else: memoir served up as fiction. And so the stories read like confessions. Because, in fact, they are.

And no one seems to have more to confess than the narrator, who is, in these pages, called "Tim O'Brien" and who is, I believe, no mere device. In 1968, O'Brien was about to graduate with honors from college in Minnesota. He had won a fellowship to Harvard. And then he was drafted.

The story that resonates most for me --- because I was also graduating from college in 1968 --- is "On the Rainy River." In it, O'Brien tries to figure out whether to flee to Canada or face his fate in Vietnam. He has a summer job in his hometown in Minnesota; abruptly, he flees and drives north, north toward the border. He gets as far as a lodge before he runs out of courage. No one is there but the aged proprietor, who instinctively knows that this young man is in the throes of crisis.

The old man doesn't invite O'Brien to talk about his "problem," in that new-fangled Oprah way. He just takes him out fishing, and pretends not to notice that O'Brien is weeping. But his silence means everything: O'Brien makes his decision, and, even more, knows why he made it.

The story ends with O'Brien driving home:

The day was cloudy. I passed through towns with familiar names, through the pine forests and down to the prairie, and then to Vietnam, where I was a soldier. I survived, but it's not a happy ending. I was a coward. I went to the war.

"I was a coward. I went to the war." That's the book in two sentences. But unlike many quickie summaries, it makes you want to read the book. ■

Jean Rhys:
"After leaving Mr. Mackenzie"

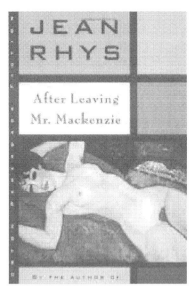

The favorite writer of Jacqueline Kennedy Onassis is said to be Jean Rhys (1890-1979). How can that be? The main characters in these novels tend to be women who are losing their ability to attract men. They drink. They live in cheap hotels.

Jean Rhys was a first-tier writer who deserves to be widely known, and I can easily understand why --- on literary grounds alone --- Mrs. Onassis would elevate her to her personal pantheon. I can also understand why Mrs. Onassis might identify with a Jean Rhys character: Mrs. Onassis was notoriously tight. I'm guessing here, but I'd bet she had an irrational fear that she had to hold on to every dollar lest she end up poor and alone --- a bag lady. She wouldn't be the first to feel this way; any number of rich people I know seem to tell themselves daily, "This could all go away."

For Julia Martin --- the main character in "After Leaving Mr. Mackenzie" (1930), probably the finest of the novels by Rhys --- it has all gone away. It's the late 1920s, and Julia's in Paris, where her nightly companion is a bottle rather than a man. Outside, there's an endless party, but she stays in her gloomy room all day, reading. And musing:

She found pleasure in memories, as an old woman might have done. Her mind was a confusion of memory and imagination. It was always places that she thought of, not people. She would lie thinking of the dark shadows of houses in a street white with sunshine; or trees with slender black branches and young green leaves, like the trees of a London square in spring; or of a dark-purple sea, the sea of a chromo or of some tropical country that she had never seen.

That burst of writing is on page 3. It is both a tour de force of insight and a warning: Rhys has an unblinking eye. What that eye sees may not be pretty --- but you can count on it to be the truth. Here is the key truth of this novel: a woman in her 30s, already looking back rather than forward. You can't help but worry for her.

Work? "By her eyes and the dark circles under them you saw that she was a dreamer, that she was vulnerable." Drunk, she looks out at the Seine and imagines it's the sea. Dear Lord, how will she make her way?

That grotty topic --- money --- is ignored in most novels. People just.... have it. Not here. Indeed, the engine of the plot of "After Leaving Mr. Mackenzie" is money. Julia lives from check to check --- on the kindness of the men who have used her and discarded her, you might say. Which is fine when the men are generous and guilty.

But now comes a lawyer's letter, with a check for 1,500 francs, five times the usual amount: This is her final payment. Mr. Mackenzie is cutting Julia off. A prudent woman would --- well, what good does it do to outline a plan of action that is unavailable to an imprudent woman like Julia? We know what Julia will do: seek Mr. Mackenzie out and have a scene. Which she does. In a restaurant. Where she ends her haughty, desperate monologue by slapping him lightly on the cheek with her glove.

Ah, but luck is with her. Reeling out of the restaurant, she encounters George Horsfield, a troubled, interior man who is attracted to birds with broken wings. Bars follow. Too many drinks. Much talk. From Mars, this could look like a mating dance.

England beckons. I can't see why --- there's nothing for Julia in London except a sister resentfully nursing their dying mother. But the change of scene energizes Julia: "She had lost the feeling of indifference to her fate, which in Paris had sustained her for so long. She knew herself ready to struggle and twist and turn, to be unscrupulous and cunning as are all weak creatures fighting for their lives against the strong."

Her mother's death triggers a complex reaction: the realization that she hates her sister (and vice versa), a sharpened resentment against the power of money, the feeling that she can almost see "the thing that was behind all this talking and posturing," a sense of herself as "a defiant flame." And on a more basic level: Can she cut a deal with George Horsfield?

Sex is ahead. Very 1920s sex --- what passes for passion in that time will be an eye-opener for some readers. And more wine. A funeral. A kind of crack-up. And, finally, the return to Paris. All along, you cannot help but think: What is it with Julia? Has she just had some bad luck and it turned her sour? Is she a selfish bitch who's getting exactly the life she deserves? Will she come to a "bad end" ---- or does her decay roll on like the Seine?

Ah, but there is Mr. Mackenzie in a cafe. This time Julia doesn't hesitate to approach him. And to ask him --- with a directness she lacked earlier --- a question. It's a short scene for an end of a book, just two quick pages. But they are so stunning they take your breath away. If you didn't know from the terse writing on every page before this that Jean Rhys is a great writer and that this, but for the grace of God, is the story of your life, you know it now. ∎

Philip Roth: "Goodbye, Columbus"

Writers don't retire. But Philip Roth did. At 79, he decided he was "finished" with fiction: "I don't want to read it, I don't want to write it, and I don't even want to talk about it anymore. It's enough!"

Maybe you've read Roth. If so, you may have read, as teenage boys do under the covers with a flashlight, his "dirtiest" book, "Portnoy's Complaint." Or "My Life As a Man." Or one of the shorter novels.

I'd lure you to Roth or remind you of his greatness with what he wrote at the beginning. His first book. The one in which we see a character who's an outsider who wants in and who sees the way there through women. Maybe I love it because I so identify.

For the reasons it won the 1960 National Book Award for fiction ... well, start with the first paragraph.

"The first time I saw Brenda she asked me to hold her glasses." That's Neil Klugman talking. He's at a swimming pool. Brenda dives, swims, returns, takes her glasses. As she moves away, "she caught the bottom of her suit between thumb and index finger and flicked what flesh had been showing back where it belonged. My blood jumped."

In 16 lines, we get the picture: young people, summer lust. In the lines that follow, the picture becomes more complex. Neil lives in Newark, with his Aunt Gladys and Uncle Max, in a crazy household where no one eats the same meal or at the same time. Brenda Patimkin lives in Short Hills --- a suburb so alien to Gladys that she uses its phone book to prop up a table.

You know where the story will go. Neil, poor, graduate of Rutgers, working at the public library, dark and Semitic, ambitious and resentful. Brenda, rich, assimilated (she's had a nose job), Radcliffe. In the heat of the summer, they'll have a romance that's largely fueled by lust.

Roth's pace and pitch are flawless. The deserted swimming pool, silver on a grey day. Long walks on suburban streets just a few hundred feet higher --- but so much cooler --- than the streets of Newark. Bowls of fruit in the Patimkins' basement refrigerator.

And, of course, The Conversation. It's about love, it's about a diaphragm, who can tell the difference? But one thing about a great writer --- he wastes nothing. That diaphragm, like a revolver in Chekhov, will return in a later act, for Brenda will leave it home when she goes back to school and her mother will find it and all hell will break loose.

Yes, in 140 pages, the question has moved far beyond summer love to the real thing --- terrible pun, and forgive me, but the rubber meets the road. The story gets resolved as we know it must. And more, it points to a future that Roth could barely imagine and that we know all about: the evolution of Neil into other first-person narrators who explore religion and status and striving in a remarkable body of work.

Philip Roth was 26 when he published "Goodbye, Columbus." A great achievement at any point in a writer's career, but as a first effort, at that tender age....and then to fill the rest of the book with five accomplished short stories....I feel like Aunt Gladys: it's hot in here, I need to sit down with a cool drink.■

James Salter: "Last Night"

I don't want to turn this into a writing class, but I want to point out a virtuoso paragraph. Subject verb object. Subject verb object. Rich in nouns, sparse on adjectives. Clean. Indeed, pristine.

Philip married Adele on a day in June. It was cloudy and the wind was blowing. Later the sun came out. It had been a while since Adele had married and she wore white: white pumps with low heels, a long white skirt that clung to her hips, a filmy blouse with a white bra underneath, and around her neck a string of freshwater pearls. They were married in her house, the one she'd gotten in the divorce. All her friends were there. She believed strongly in friendship. The room was crowded.

"Prose like a windowpane," said Orwell, who also wrote this way. The writer puts you in the room, lets you watch, keeps out of your way. What the characters say and do matters --- the writer doesn't.

Who are these characters? White. Educated. Moneyed. "Philip was mannerly and elegant, his head held back a bit as he talked, as though you were a menu." And Adele? "Out of the afternoon haze she would appear, in her black bathing suit, limbs all tan, the brilliant sun behind her. She was the strong figure walking up the smooth sand from the sea, her legs, her wet swimmer's hair, the grace of her, all careless and unhurried."

But Salter doesn't dwell on happiness.

"He didn't make much money, as it turned out. He wrote for a business weekly. She earned nearly that much selling houses. She had begun to put on a little weight. This was a few years after they were married. She was still beautiful --- her face was --- but she had adopted a more comfortable outline."

Whew. That was fast. And efficient: "This was a few years after they were married."

Oh, there's liquor. You knew these people would drink, sometimes too much. Adele does. And says more than is discreet. Philip walks outside, sees a comet. Adele joins him. She has no interest in the comet. She goes inside. As he watches, she trips on the kitchen steps. And that's all. Gossamer.

You could say: "This isn't a story, it's a sketch." And you'd have a point. But the thing about Salter is that he shows you only what's needed, then invites you to imagine the rest. When I think of Salter, I'm reminded of John Updike's remark, "A psychoanalyst talking is like playing golf on the moon --- even a chip shot carries for miles." Salter hits chip shots.

Many will find this writing overly mannered. Yes, there are crumpled napkins on tables uncleared from last night's dinner party: "glasses still with dark remnant on them, coffee stains, and plates with bits of hardened Brie." Privileged women pine for love -- or sex. At a man's funeral, there are women the widow has never seen before. A married man is having an affair with a male friend. A hill is made from a pile of junked cars. A romantic opportunity is missed.

Salter is too discreet to shove the engine room of life into our faces, but it's very much there. One story ends with a woman dying of cancer --- a young woman. Another focuses on an older woman on what is to be the final night of her life: "She had a face now that was for the afterlife and those she would meet there."

The sentences drop, regular as coins. Salter's cadences are so hypnotic it's easy to miss them. But they are arrows to the real subject of these stories, which are, like the best stories about adult men and women, about honor and love in the face of death.

132 pages. Ten stories. They may read like trifles, like exercises, like parlor tricks --- but you can't forget them. Could it be because they are small masterpieces? ∎

Anna Sewell: "Black Beauty"

The last book Ludwig Wittgenstein read --- the book he read as he lay dying --- was "Black Beauty."

For decades, I wondered why.

Wittgenstein was arguably the greatest philosopher of the 20th Century. Although he wrote that "Everything that can be said can be said clearly," his linguistic analysis is brainsplittingly difficult. By all accounts, doing philosophy was torment for him. Why, of all the books he knew, would he turn in his final days to a book we think of as a novel for children?

I wanted to know the answer, so I re-read "Black Beauty." And at last I think I see what the lure was for Wittgenstein --- "Black Beauty" is not a book for kids, it's a parable for us all.

As a child in the 1800s, Sewell injured her leg and was an invalid for life. Because she lived with her mother in London, she had more reasons than most to use horse-drawn carriages. There were as many as 10,000 hansom cabs in London at that time; many of the horses were badly treated.

"Black Beauty" was Sewell's only book. She wrote it in the last few years of her life, when she was so weak she had to dictate it to her mother. But she was as clear a thinker as she was a storyteller. Her aim in writing "Black Beauty," she said, was to "induce kindness, sympathy and an understanding of the treatment of horses." She succeeded admirably. "Black Beauty" was an instant hit, and is said to be "the sixth best seller in the English language." Sewell died a few months after it was published. I would say her life was complete.

And I would say that Black Beauty's life is complete as well. As he tells the story --- remember, the horse is the narrator --- animals are just people in other forms. They think, feel, speak. And their personalities are a sophisticated combination of temperament and circumstance.

The real subject of the novel, I would suggest, is time --- and how it brings change. Black Beauty has great luck in his youth; his mother is a good teacher and his master is kind. He learns not to be afraid of trains, to be a good partner to another horse as they pull a carriage.

Black Beauty offers occasional advice: "If people knew what a comfort to horses a light hand is, and how it keeps a good mouth and a good temper, they surely would not chuck, and drag, and pull at the rein as they often do." Just the sort of reminder you might be tempted to leave --- anonymously --- on the desk of a heavy-handed, meddling, micro-managing boss, don't you think?

Black Beauty has speed, and in an emergency, he can get a messenger to a doctor fast enough to save his mistress's life. He has great instincts, and refuses to cross a rotting bridge, saving more lives. He is loved and thanked, fed well and expertly cared for; his lot could not be better.

But three years of happiness are all Black Beauty has, for his owner must move to a better climate and his horses must be sold. Misuse leads to injury, and Black Beauty leaves the world of country privilege for the city life. But it is not so bad; his master is kindness incarnate. Among Jerry's beliefs: "If we see cruelty or wrong that we have the power to stop, and we do nothing, we make ourselves sharers in the guilt." (Gee, see any implications there?)

Seeing is believing? The horse knows better: "Feeling is believing." And as he falls to the lowest rung, he comes to learn what real cruelty is like. Oh, but this is a Victorian story --- it must end well. And it does. The circle is completed. In his old age, Black Beauty is returned to his rightful prominence. "My troubles are over." Before he is quite awake, he often finds himself dreaming of his first home....

Yes, I think I understand why Wittgenstein read "Black Beauty" at the end. It's a picture of an orderly world, and good that has power over evil. It's a world anyone would want to live in. And, with this book in hand for a few hours, anyone can. ∎

PETER TEMPLE: "TRUTH"

Laurie doesn't see him, so Steve Villani is able to study his wife as she walks toward him.

Jeans, black leather jacket, thinner, different haircut, a more confident stride.

She spots him, comes over.

He hasn't planned it, but he can't help himself. "You're having an affair."

She says this isn't the place to talk. He won't let it go.

"Fuck meeting with the boyfriend, is that it?"

"I'm not having an affair," she says. "I'm in love with someone, I'll move out today."

Looking for great fiction-writing? Friends, that is it: not a word wasted, every beat true, drama at the red line, a surprise that packs a wallop.

What more do you want? Whatever your fantasy about a book, Peter Temple probably satisfies it in "Truth." Peter Temple? Only one of the world's better novelists. But unknown to most American readers largely because he lives in Australia.

Temple is underappreciated here for another reason: His books are thrillers with violent crimes as the problem to be solved and cops as the characters who must solve them. In our country, that's the province of genre specialists like Patricia Cornwell and James Patterson — writers who favor simple plots, cardboard dialogue and lots of white space on the page. Temple, in comparison, is Dostoevsky.

The comparison is not casual. Temple's characters are complex, his plots complicated, his world smudged if not outright dirty — that is, his books are entirely credible. In this one, a young prostitute is found murdered in a super-luxury high rise that boasts the ultimate in technology — though on the night of the murder, none of it works. In Temple's books, high and low always meet. Not only might the murder be connected to the torture and execution of three thugs, but Steve Villani, chief of the Homicide squad in Melbourne, must deal with citizens of every caste.

He's having an affair, for instance, with a successful TV newscaster. He's invited to a party given by a gazillionaire, where he recognizes "a millionaire property owner, an actor whose career was dead, a famous footballer you could rent by the hour, two cocaine-addicted television personalities, a sallow man who owned racehorses and many jockeys." And, when it's time to be a tough cop, he can go there: "He fell sideways and Villani stopped him meeting the concrete, not with love, laid him to rest, put a shoe on his chest, rested his weight, moved it up to the windpipe and pressed, tapped, you did not want to mark the cunt."

If the plot has more layers than a Goldman Sachs bond deal, it's fun to try and figure out what's coming. (Good luck.) What's simple — and simply delightful — is Temple's dialogue, which verges on shorthand.

Here he is, giving a deputy his marching orders for the daily media update on the prostitute's murder:

"Take the media gig this afternoon?"
"Well, yes, certainly. Yes."
"Give them the waffle. Can't name Ribarics. On the torture, it's out there, so the line is horrific and so on. We're shocked. Scumbags' inhumanity to other filth. With me?"
"Urge people to come forward?"
"Mate, absolutely. In large numbers."

And here, in a scene so emotionally rewarding you'll want to give Villani a fist-pump, is the Homicide chief grilling a high government official who just happened to have been the young prostitute's final client:

"Are we done?" said Koenig. "I'm a busy man."
"Not done, no, not at all," said Villani. "But we can conduct this interview in other circumstances."
"Is that, we can do this here or we can do it at the station? Jesus, what a cliché."
"That's what we deal in," said Villani.
"I'm a minister of the crown, you grasped that, detective?"
"I'm an inspector. From Homicide. Didn't I say that?"

Fun, but never charming. This is, after all, Homicide, "where animals hated you, dreamed of revenge, would kill your family." It's a job that eats you, "your family got the tooth-scarred bone." A job where crimes are sometimes solved by looking at footage taken by a security camera at night and noticing the reflection of a car's license plate on a window, and sometimes solved in nastier ways.

You want validation? Try this: In 2010, "Truth" won the Miles Franklin Literary Award, the most prestigious literary prize in Australia. Funded by the author of "My Brilliant Career," it's awarded to "the novel of the year which is of the highest literary merit and presents Australian life in any of its phases." To quote the judges: "'Truth' disorients the reader with multiple plots and elliptical exchanges: blank spaces occupy almost as much room on the page as the print. In this way Temple takes a popular genre and transforms it into a radical literary experiment in realism and fiction. There is minimal exposition of plot and character; rather the narrative is embedded in voice and dialogue rich with colloquialisms and police lingo, heard in grabs from radio, in cars, on mobile phones, and in conversations across always crowded rooms. We learn to trust the accumulation of fragments and scenes. Few contemporary fiction writers grasp the speech and silences of the Australian vernacular as effectively as Temple."

You want a mindless beach read? Skip this. You want to be bitch-slapped into full attention by a master? Come ahead.■

WALTER TEVIS:
"THE QUEEN'S GAMBIT"

On a long plane trip, I started reading "The Queen's Gambit," by Walter Tevis, author of "The Man Who Fell to Earth" and "The Hustler." I had read none of those books. Nor had I seen the movies made from them. I just had a hunch.

I was never smarter --- this is a novel that, very simply, cannot be put down. The woman who would become my first wife tried to make conversation; I shushed her. A meal came; I pushed it aside. All I could do was read, straight to the end --- weeping, cheering, punching the air.

I got off the plane and optioned the film rights to "Queen's Gambit," and was soon at work on the greatest script I will probably ever undertake. Every young actress wanted to star in it, a half dozen "hot" directors wanted to direct it. Then the parade moved on. I couldn't afford to keep the option. Walter Tevis died. His widow, needing money, sold the movie rights to people who, in 25 years, have not been able to get the film made. The book went out of print.

Two decades later, a paperback edition appeared. No Kindle; the publisher is asleep.

What's the fuss about? An eight-year-old orphan named Beth Harmon. Who turns out to be the Mozart of chess. Which brings her joy (she wins! people notice her!) and misery (she's alone and unloved and incapable of asking for help). So she gets addicted to pills. She drinks. She loses. And then, as 17-year-old Beth starts pulling herself together, she must face the biggest challenge of all --- a match with the world champion, a Russian of scary brilliance.

You think: This is thrilling? You think: chess? You think: Must be an "arty" novel, full of interior scenes.

Wrong. All wrong. "The Queen's Gambit" is "Rocky."

But here is the catch. Although this is a very adult book --- what is more grown up than the realization that we cannot really succeed in life, no matter how "gifted" we may be, if we are alone and unloved? --- it is so artlessly written it seems almost to have no style. This is the dream novel: 100% story.

Here, for example, is Beth, freshly orphaned, breaking through her shyness to confront the silent giant of a custodian who spends his days playing solitary chess in the orphanage's furnace room:

"Will you teach me?"
Mr. Shaibel said nothing, did not even register the question with a movement of his head. Distant voices from above were singing "Bringing in the Sheaves."
She waited for several minutes. Her voice almost broke with the effort of her words, but she pushed them out, anyway: "I want to learn to play chess."
Mr. Shaibel reached out a fat hand to one of the larger black pieces, picked it up deftly by its head and set it down on a square at the other side of the board. He brought the hand back and folded his arms across his chest. He still did not look at Beth. "I don't play strangers."
The flat voice had the effect of a slap in the face. Beth turned and left, walking upstairs with the bad taste in her mouth.
"I'm not a stranger," she said to him two days later. "I live here." Behind her head a small moth circled the bare bulb, and its pale shadow crossed the board at regular intervals. "You can teach me. I already know some of it, from watching."
"Girls don't play chess." Mr. Shaibel's voice was flat.
She steeled herself and took a step closer, pointing at, but not touching, one of the cylindrical pieces that she had already labeled a cannon in her imagination."This one moves up and down or back and forth. All the way, if there's space to move in."
Mr. Shaibel was silent for a while. Then he pointed at the one with what looked like a slashed lemon on top. "And this one?"
Her heart leapt. "On the diagonals."

See? You don't need to know anything about chess. Tevis was a storyteller whose genius was to tell great stories; there's nothing between you and the people.

I believe that you will care about Beth Harmon more than any fictional character you've encountered in years and years.

I believe that you will grasp the wrench of loneliness --- and the power of love --- as if this book were happening to you.

And I believe that you will weep, and cheer, and, at the end, raise your fist like a fool for a little girl who never existed and a game only nerds play. ∎

KURT VONNEGUT:
"SLAUGHTERHOUSE-FIVE"

Kurt Vonnegut was born on November 11, 1922, exactly four years after the end of World War I. On Mother's Day in 1944, while he was home on leave from the Army, his mother killed herself.

A year later, Vonnegut was a prisoner of war in Dresden when Allied bombers firebombed the city, killing 135,000 people --- more dead than from the two atomic bombs dropped on Japan. And just for icing on that tower of irony: Decades later, his sister Alice died from cancer just hours after her husband died in a train crash.

From those facts alone, you could imagine going through life with a permanent smirk and a never-ending shrug. Or just taking to bed.

Instead, Kurt Vonnegut wrote a series of books that have established him as a national treasure, a 20th Century Mark Twain. His vision is all-seeing, but his touch is gentle. He leaves religion for suckers, but he preaches the gospel of love and forgiveness. He taught writing at prestigious institutions, but his own work is shot through with characters and themes from science fiction, a lowbrow genre. And although he didn't write lurid sex or racy dialogue, his books have a nasty habit of being banned --- in the early '70s in North Dakota, they actually burned copies of "Slaughterhouse-Five."

Well, that's just some of the title. The rest: "The Children's Crusade: A Duty-Dance with Death, by Kurt Vonnegut, Jr., a Fourth-Generation German-American Now Living in Easy Circumstances on Cape Cod (and Smoking Too Much) Who, as an American Infantry Scout Hors de Combat, as a Prisoner of War, Witnessed the Fire-Bombing of Dresden, Germany, the Florence of the Elbe, a Long Time Ago, and Survived to Tell the Tale: This Is a Novel Somewhat in the Telegraphic Schizophrenic Manner of Tales of the Planet Tralfamadore, Where The Flying Saucers Come From."

Yes, you could see how just that would upset someone with a strict regard for titles and subtitles. Or even for plots, which are not Vonnegut's apparent strength: Vonnegut likes to set up a situation and then digress. He does what you're never supposed to: talk directly to the reader. He introduces characters from his own life --- in the books, he is sometimes a character named "Kurt Vonnegut."

So it really won't help you if I relate what happens in "Slaughterhouse-Five." I mean: Billy Pilgrim is unstuck in time. A hundred words (or more) won't clear that up. And even judicious quoting won't convey the charm of Vonnegut to those who haven't read him. And if I tell you the "message" of this book --- "Be kind. Don't hurt. Death is coming for all of us anyway, and it is better to be Lot's wife looking back through salty eyes than the Deity that destroyed those cities of the plain in order to save them" --- I'm not going to advance your understanding much.

But there is one passage in "Slaughterhouse-Five" that is widely quoted, and it's the sort of thing only Kurt Vonnegut would write. If you've missed this masterpiece, maybe these words will convince you to try "Slaughterhouse-Five." If not, as Vonnegut says often in these pages, "So it goes." Anyway, here:

American planes, full of holes and wounded men and corpses, took off backwards from an airfield in England. Over France, a few German fighter planes flew at them backwards, sucked bullets and shell fragments from some of the planes and crewmen. . . .The bombers opened their bomb-bay doors, exerted a miraculous magnetism which shrunk the fires, gathered them into cylindrical steel containers, and lifted the containers into the bellies of the planes. The Germans below had miraculous devices of their own, which were long steel tubes. They used them to suck more fragments from the crewmen and planes.

When the bombers got back to their base, the steel cylinders were taken from the racks and snipped back to the United States of America, where factories were operating night and day, dismantling the cylinders, separating the dangerous contents into minerals. Touchingly, it was mainly women who did this work. The minerals were then shipped to specialists in remote areas. It was their business to put them into the ground, to hide them cleverly, so they would never hurt anybody ever again.

Lovely thought. Lovely man. Books like no other.■

Jess Walter:
"Beautiful Ruins"

I don't lose books. But we were at a hotel in Las Vegas with a wave pool, it was 101 degrees and umbrellas cost $100. There were women with tattoos everywhere: their backs, their legs, their arms. With all that ink, could you remember to take a mere book from under your chaise?

To my astonishment, no one in this crowd turned "Beautiful Ruins" in to Lost & Found.

So I bought it again.

I soon understood why anyone who found it would have held on to it --- it's a stunner. Or, as they'd say at the wave pool, awesome. Very unique. A real journey of a novel.

And it's not just one literate Vegas vacationer who thinks so. Richard Russo, no slouch as a novelist, and I agree: "Why mince words? 'Beautiful Ruins' is an absolute masterpiece."

Masterpiece. A work of high quality made by a master. In this case, Jess Walter. (I'd read not a word of his until this, but his books are consistently honored: Time Magazine's #2 novel of the year, finalist for the National Book Award, winner of the LA Times Book Prize, winner of the Edgar Allan Poe Award for best novel, New York Times notable book.) Born in Spokane, he lives in Spokane. And yet he's written the wisest, worldliest novel I've read this year.

What's it about? Italy in the 1960s, Hollywood in the 1960s, Hollywood now, World War II, the set of "Cleopatra," the Donner party, World War II, Seattle, the Edinburgh Fringe Festival, Idaho --- but this long list is scaring you, yes?

If the locations aren't daunting, the massive cast might make you nervous: the proprietor of the Hotel Adequate View, a six room, three table nothing of a resort in an Italian coastal town only accessible by boat, Richard Burton and Elizabeth Taylor, a Hollywood publicist turned producer, a novelist who can't get beyond the first chapter, an unproduced screenwriter, a singer-comic, an assistant film executive whose boyfriend can be found at strip clubs, and --- I almost forgot --- the woman who seems to be at the center of all this, a young American actress named Dee Moray, who was briefly in "Cleopatra" and has come to this nowhere hotel because she's been told she's dying of cancer.

Too busy for you? And when I confess that the novel jumps around in time, do you feel you will be confused? In lesser hands, you would be. But this is a masterpiece, remember? Fifteen years in the making, many drafts.

"Beautiful Ruins" is, by turns, funny, tragic, satirical. Like life, it is always surprising. Like life, it has threads that connect unlikely people --- but only in retrospect. Like life, victories are hard-won, defeats are learning experiences. And better than life, it all makes sense in the end.

I won't quote it; it's too hard to isolate what's great about this novel. Because it all is. Every sentence. I know: That's crazy talk. But "Beautiful Ruins" is one of those reading experiences that delights and challenges you along the way, thrills you often, and, at the end, makes you cry --- well, makes *me* cry --- for a world glorious enough for these characters and this writer. ∎

EDITH WHARTON:
"THE HOUSE OF MIRTH"

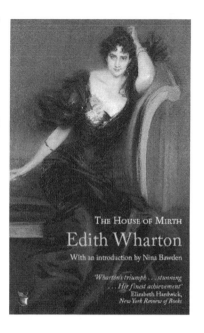

Lawrence Selden was infatuated with Lily Bart. She was from a good family. And beautiful. And special: "He had a confused sense that she must have cost a great deal to make, that a great many dull and ugly people must, in some mysterious way, have been sacrificed to produce her."

What's wrong with Lily Bart? Just three things. Her family has lost its money. She's unmarried. And she's 29.

Twenty-nine and unmarried --- that's far from a tragedy today, though there's always some fool around to remind a single woman that her biological clock is ticking. But in 1903 to 1905, when Edith Wharton was writing "The House of Mirth," society --- that is, upper-class New York "Society" --- was remarkably judgmental about a woman in such a position.

Particularly if she had lost her inheritance, as Lily has. Because, in that circumstance, she was prey to rich, married men who wanted to "help" her in exchange for the kind of thanks that permanently destroys a woman's reputation.

That is the conflict of Wharton's first great novel: a woman fighting to make her way through a Society infused with more hypocrisy than humanity. This is high-toned stuff, not raw material for popular fiction. But Wharton saw a way. "A frivolous society can acquire dramatic significance," she explained, "only through what its frivolity destroys."

How modern this all is. Lily's beauty is "an asset." Her character flaws are common ones: "The only problems she could not solve were those with which she was familiar." And Selden --- do we not know at least one decent, intelligent, mild-mannered young man who could brighten the light in a woman's eyes if he weren't working so hard, if he could just stop being so damned decent?

The reason "House of Mirth" is assigned in English class is because it is a brilliantly written dissection of a society we like to think has disappeared. How dreary. And how...wrong. The reason to read it is because only the particulars have changed.

The essential questions of the drama are as interesting now as they were compelling then: What will happen to Lily Bart? Will Selden rescue her? Or will rich married men ruin her? And if she is ruined, what will happen to her then?

Wharton learned her craft from de Maupassant, and her book is such great visual storytelling that to read it is, in a sense, to see the movie. So don't think you'll pick it up to improve your mind. This is popular fiction at its best: pure, nail-biting pleasure. ■

BOOKS

HISTORY

MILTON MAYER:
"THEY THOUGHT THEY WERE FREE:
THE GERMANS, 1933-1945"

n 1935, a Jewish reporter from Chicago went to Germany in the hopes of interviewing Adolph Hitler. That didn't happen, so he traveled around the country. What he saw surprised him: Nazism wasn't "the tyranny of a diabolical few over helpless millions" --- it was a mass movement.

In 1951, the Jewish reporter from Chicago returned to Germany. This time Milton Mayer had a different goal: to interview ten Nazis so thoroughly he felt he really knew them. Only then, he believed, might he understand how it came to be that the Germans exterminated millions of their fellow citizens.

He found ten Germans. And interviewed them at such length they became his friends. Reading his daughter's memories of her father, I can understand how that happened. "His German was awful!" wrote Julie Mayer Vogner. "And this was a great aid in the interviews he conducted: having to repeat, in simpler words, or more slowly, what they had to say made the Germans he was interviewing feel relaxed, equal to, superior to the interviewer, and this made them speak more freely."

In 1955, Mayer published "They Thought They Were Free: The Germans, 1933-45." It was a disturbing book then. It still is. For one thing, Mayer had only the warmest feelings for the men he interviewed:

I liked them. I couldn't help it. Again and again, as I sat or walked with one or another of my ten [Nazi] friends, I was overcome by the same sensation that had got in the way of my newspaper reporting in Chicago years before [in the 1930s]. I liked Al Capone. I liked the way he treated his mother. He treated her better than I treated mine.

The ten interviewees were quite the diverse crew: a janitor, soldier, cabinetmaker, Party headquarters office manager, baker, bill collector, high school teacher, high school student, policeman, Labor front inspector.

"These ten men were not men of distinction," Mayer notes. "They were not opinion makers.... In a nation of seventy million, they were the sixty-nine million plus. They were the Nazis, the little men..."

What didn't they know, and when didn't they know it?

They did not know before 1933 that Nazism was evil. They did not know between 1933 and 1945 that it was evil. And they do not know it now [in 1951]. None of them ever knew, or now knows, Nazism as we knew it, and know it; and they lived under it, served it, and, indeed, made it.

And none ever thought Hitler would lead them into war.

Why not?

– They had never traveled abroad.
– They didn't talk to foreigners or read the foreign press.
– Before Hitler, most had no jobs. Now they did.
– The targets of their hatred had been stigmatized well in advance of any action against them.
– They really weren't asked to "do" anything — just not to interfere.
– The men who burned synagogues did not live in the cities of the synagogues.
– Hitler was a father figure, right to the end. (He was "betrayed" by his subordinates.)

The more you read, the more your jaw drops. How many people did it require to take over a country? "A few hundred at the top, to plan and direct.... a few thousand to supervise and control.... a few score thousand specialists, eager to serve...a million to do the dirty work...."

There's more, much more. Some of it is quite specific to the German character (yes, there apparently are national characteristics). And some of it might stand as universal metaphor. If you're not a history buff, that's the reason to read this book --- it's a revealing study of "little" people, people who seem insignificant, good citizens who do as they're told.

Who knew nobodies could be so important --- or so dangerous? ∎

BOOKS

MEMOIR

Michael Arlen:
"Exiles"

The photograph on the cover doesn't suggest how short they both were, how small. All you notice is her pleated skirt just so, his hands shoved casually in the jacket pockets of his natty double-breasted suit. They look confident, elegant.

But there's something the photo doesn't catch. Michael Arlen --- author of a novel called "The Green Hat" --- may be more successful than his friends F. Scott Fitzgerald and Ernest Hemingway. But Michael Arlen isn't who he looks like; he was born Dikran Kouyoumdjian, an Armenian. In London, he won't fit in. Ditto in New York and the South of France. And his wife isn't exactly who she looks like either.

Exiles. So their son, Michael J. Arlen, thinks of them. Exiles? How can that be --- they had it all. Michael Arlen's photograph was on the cover of Time Magazine. In the South of France, he owned the very best speedboat and hired a driver for it. Willie Maugham and Winston Churchill came for lunch. "The day he arrived in Chicago, the Daily News ran a front-page story --- saying that he had arrived in Chicago." But when the fame went away, he was beached.

Michael J. Arlen gets the glitter. And, even more, the courage that kept his father going. He tells the delicious story of his father running into Louis B. Mayer, the movie mogul, at the "21" Club in New York. Arlen had just arrived from England; Mayer asked about his plans. "I was just talking to Sam Goldwyn," Arlen said --- which was true, he'd just encountered Mayer's rival, who had urged him to buy horses. Mayer asked, "How much did he offer you?" Arlen thought fast: "Not enough." A few minutes later, he had a 30-week contract as a writer at MGM for $1,500 a week.

Michael Arlen wants to be a father to his son, so he invites the boy out to California. There's a weekend in Santa Barbara. At Clark Gable's house. Only Gable's not there. It's a house party of tanned men and attractive women. Of cigarettes and liquor. And a terrible moment when his father is talking --- and nobody's listening. Later, the boy finds his father sitting by the pool. "I was out here a long time ago," his father said. "We used to play tennis. Thalberg --- he always wanted to talk about literature."

These are people of a breed long vanished, and their lives will seem strange. The big duplex apartment. Long lunches. Cocktail time. Sitting in the library at night, reading and drinking. And the sadness: young Michael hearing his father in the afternoon, not writing, just pacing, pacing. Here's his mother, dying, her last words coming across decades, from Monte Carlo: "Let's take the road down by the sea this time. It will be longer, but nothing really starts until ten anyway..."

Other stories are right out of Salinger or John O'Hara. Young Michael, at boarding school, not winning and then winning a history prize. Michael, a senior at Harvard, desperate to marry his 19-year-old girlfriend. Their parents don't approve. Oh, the agony, "the back-seat-of-the car fifteen floors above Park Avenue." And, a little later, Michael, frustrated, making a phone call and getting a job in the Henry Luce empire.

I haven't mentioned the writing. I think this book is right up there with the stories of James Salter, but some will find it falsely casual, like talking, but like a very self-conscious voice talking. Maybe. Consider where Michael J. Arlen came from. And consider, too, that this is an elegy, and elegies should shine. Like this:

They were both of them beautiful. They were also, both of them, in a kind of exile, and sought to find a home, a country, in one another, and very nearly did, came as close to it as maybe it is possible to do, but they were each so deep in exile when they met --- and how would they have known that? My mother, so seemingly established --- a title, even, money somewhere in the background, big houses, gardens, furniture, wax for the furniture, polish for the silver, manners, style, and more than manners or style, a seeming feel for independence.... and seeking to escape from her (still unknown) exile, from all those mannered, self-protective people into this unusual man's vitality, life, imagination, energy --- well, as with many men, it turned out to be a fragile, an especially fragile kind of energy. So delicate, really. Too delicate. But that was for later, for much later. It was later that they found these things out, or didn't find them out, just lived them, lived under them. In the beginning, though, it must have been lovely....

Tastes differ. But this writing never fails to thrill me.■

Edmund de Waal:
"The Hare with Amber Eyes"

There are men and women who write beautifully, every word inevitable, the paragraphs building into chapters, the chapters adding up to a great book, and we never suspect that their work is a phenomenal trick --- that they bled over every word, turned every sentence around a dozen times, missed meals with their children, sacrificing all to make their writing look effortless.

And then there are men and women who write beautifully because they're tuned to a different frequency and do everything beautifully. They may work to make their writing better, but they're starting at such a high level they really don't need to --- they're in humanity's elite.

Edmund de Waal is in that second group. And so we start with an irony --- the author of the most exquisite memoir you're likely to read this year isn't a writer. He's a potter, said to be one of the best in England, and Professor of Ceramics at the University of Westminster.

You could say the eye that judges a pot is also a writer's eye.

And you could say a gifted Brit who studied English at Cambridge really should be able to write a compelling family story.

But none of that would explain the fierce attachment that readers of "The Hare with Amber Eyes" have for it, why they can't help talking about it, why they press copies on friends.

Let me try. Start here: "The Hare with Amber Eyes" has, as they say in show biz, *everything.* The highest echelons of Society in pre-World War I Paris. Nazi thugs and Austrian collaborators. A gay heir who takes refuge in Japan. Style. Seduction. Rothschild-level wealth. Two centuries of anti-Semitism. And 264 pieces of netsuke, the pocket-sized ivory-or-wood sculpture first made in Japan in the 17th century.

It's on netsuke that de Waal hangs his tale --- or, rather, searches for it. Decades after he apprenticed as a potter in Japan, he has returned to research his mentor. In the

In the afternoons, he makes pots. And, one afternoon a week, he visits his great-uncle Iggie.

Iggie owns a large vitrine, in which he displays his netsuke collection. He has stories about that collection, but then he has so many tales about his family that de Waal delightedly spoons them up --- glorious anecdotes of hunting parties in Czechoslovakia, gypsies with dancing bears, his grandmother bringing special cakes from Vienna on the Orient Express. And then this:

And Emmy pulling him from the window at breakfast to show him an autumnal tree outside the dining room window covered in goldfinches. And how when he knocked on the window and they flew, the tree was still blazing golden.

I shivered when I read that last sentence --- you don't often read a description of real-world magic expressed so magically. And so simply!

All week long, I open books, hoping for a line like that. Mostly, I get well-intentioned banality --- the world viewed through eyes dulled by experience. Bu de Waal is a visual artist; he lives to look, and look hard. And, like a detective, he'll keep looking until he's put the objects of his interest into a kind of order.

His interest: the collection of netsuke bought in 1870 in Paris by Charles Ephrussi, a cousin of his great-grandfather. Because his family is "staggeringly rich," Charles is able to exercise his considerable taste. No holding back with this collector --- in the best story about Charles, he buys a still life of asparagus from Manet at a price so over-the-top that the artist sends a unique thank-you: a painting of a single stalk of asparagus, with a note, "This seems to have slipped from the bundle."

Charles in Paris: a city of salons, exquisite clothes, complicated relationships. The world of Proust. It's no surprise that Charles and Marcel were friends or that the novelist based a character on him.

"I have fallen for Charles," de Waal writes. Yes, he has, and it shows; there's more here about Charles than most readers will want. Feel free to skim. Skip, if you must. But don't, for the sake of your immortal soul, put the book down, for in 1899, Charles sends his first cousin in Vienna the netsuke as a wedding present and the book goes into a different gear.

In Vienna, de Waal writes, there were 145,000 Jews in 1899 --- 71 per cent of the city's financiers, 65 per cent of the lawyers, 59 per cent of the doctors, half the journalists. Why does he begin this chapter by telling us about the Jews when, as he notes, they were so assimilated? Oh, you know why; it just takes three-and-a-half decades for the anti-Semitism he chronicles to reach a boil.

I've studied World War I, as you have, but not from the point-of-view of a rich

Jews who owned palaces were exempt. So you will encounter nail-biting terror here. And you'll be brought up short: How did a book about a collection of objects take such a radical turn? And how, amid the horror, did 264 pieces of netsuke survive intact?

England, Japan, Russia. The research unhinges de Waal: "I no longer know if this book is about my family, or memory, or myself, or if it is a book about small Japanese things." Curiously, that is to the book's advantage; it's really up to the reader to take what meaning he or she can from this story of objects gained, lost, found.

What are objects to us? Do they change when we hold them, display them, give them value? Do they "retain the pulse of their makeup?" If we didn't collect anything, how would we remember who we were?

Edmund de Waal and his wife live with their three young children --- and the vitrine of netsuke. The kids sometimes play with the little pieces. "But there is no aesthetic life with small kids around," de Waal has told interviewers. "They want that plastic tiara, or Disney water pistol --- and you remember what it is to start accumulating things in your life." The implication is clear: Eventually those kids will understand and appreciate what it means to hold the objects of their ancestors.

My ancestors are dust. At most, there are a few photographs. So for me, the moral of this book is that everything matters but nothing lasts. Cherish beauty, but keep it private. And, if you are a Jew, always be prepared to pack and flee on an hour's notice.

Your take will be just as personal. And you might as well accept that going in --- this is not a book about Japanese art objects. ∎

Mary Karr: "Lit"

A lot has happened in Mary Karr's life, almost all of it colorful, much of it painful. And in each of her three books, she's followed the advice of her mentor Tobias Wolff ("Take no care for your dignity") and produced not just a bestseller, but a memoir that expands our idea of what a memoir is.

If you missed "The Liar's Club" or "Cherry," "Lit" offers a cheat sheet. Raised in Port Arthur, Texas by a father who worked --- literally --- in oil and a flighty, unstable mother who, one especially dark night, was intent on killing her daughters with a knife, Karr bailed on her family when she was 17. In California, she did menial work and learned to drink. But she knew that writing was her destiny, and she honed a style of poetry that stripped language clean in order to deliver taut, blunt stories.

She got noticed --- especially by a tall, Harvard-educated poet. They married and had a son, and, right there, when it looked as if she had everything, she started downing a bottle of Jack Daniels a day. It wasn't as if she didn't recognize the trouble she was in. Alcohol flowed through her family history --- her father, she's written, could start a fight sitting alone on the front porch. But she was desperately afraid her husband would divorce her and win custody of their son.

"Lit" is about many things: the resolution of her relationship with her mother and father, her struggle for recognition as a writer, her inability to unfreeze her marriage. But mostly it's about alcohol and faith --- about an intellectually arrogant woman who's too proud to surrender and too smart to believe. In the last half of her book, she does both.

The image of Mary Karr at AA meetings and on her knees in prayer is a stunner. The release from alcohol, hard as it was, is the lesser miracle for her. The greater surprise? Her embrace of Catholicism.

JK: In the past year, I've read memoirs or novels by female alcoholics --- Caroline Knap, Michelle Huneven, Kaylie Jones, Gail Caldwell --- and now you. What is it about women and alcohol that leads to writing?

MK: Sorry, but I think my alcoholism was at most 20% of "Lit." Writers have been alcoholics since time immemorial. But only now are many writing about it. And you have to make a distinction between literature and sound-byte memoirs. The sound-byte memoir is only worth reading in an airport. I want to create a whole world, like a novel.

JK: Of your drinking before you started living with Warren, the patrician poet who'd become your husband, you write, "So long as I didn't leave my apartment, I didn't drink." Why?

MK: Because if went anywhere, I'd get shitfaced drunk or take any cocaine proffered. So I had to stay in the house, go to the library and school, and come right home --- that was my world. One night I went to an art opening where I knew there would be really shitty white wine --- and I got shattered.

JK: What is alcoholism to you --- a disease, chemical condition or a learned response?

MK: I buy the disease model because it makes it easiest for me to stay sober. And at the end of drinking, you do feel compelled. I mean, I don't lack for self-discipline. I floss. I do sit ups. I pay taxes. I do all kinds of shit I don't want to do. But if a drink's around...

JK: Okay, let's deal with this religious conversion of yours. In your childhood, you write, the bookstore in Port Arthur sold gold-rimmed Bibles and dashboard Christs...

MK: ...and I was completely immune to religion. I thought it was like the Easter bunny. I was in the 5th grade before I got that people were serious about God --- I thought the whole thing was a social convention. I had no idea people believed this made-up stuff.

JK: Your mother never said a word about God?

MK: Mother was a spiritual dilettante. Gods came and went --- Theosophy, yoga in the early sixties, Zen, Christian Science. I'd say our religious education interested her less than our artistic one, but she didn't pay much attention. To Mother, we were like lizards in a terrarium. Once a week she'd tap the glass and see if we were still moving.

JK: I'm a believer of sorts, but reading the story of your religious conversion was like a horror movie. I kept wanting to scream, "Turn back!"

MK: And it was just like that. It's like: You don't want to be a werewolf, but you wake up in a field wearing a cloak of muslin and fur wrapped around your head.

JK: I have trouble picturing Mary Karr going through the alphabet, giving thanks letter by letter.

MK: I was desperate, and it was like they were pointing to a stump and saying, Talk to that; or to a tailor's dummy and saying, That's your prom date. But faith is not a feeling. It's a set of actions. Prayer was 100% rote for me, but I'd beaten myself into this teachable state. I could finally get that my life was warped and my thoughts were way off. And the woman who told me to pray my way through the alphabet was a Harvard social theorist who'd written a famous book on Durkheim. At first I complained, so she made me read my gratitude list to her on the phone. Which was smart --- a lot of times it's just doing what you're told, it's not about the beliefs. And now religion is a necessity. I didn't have a choice. I had to get religion.

JK: In Graham Greene's "End of the Affair", there's this passage: "I believe there's a God --- I believe the whole bag of tricks, there's nothing I don't believe, they could subdivide the Trinity into a dozen parts and I'd believe. They could dig up reasons that proved Christ had been invented by Pilate to get himself promoted and I'd believe just the same. I've caught belief like a disease. I've fallen into belief like I fell in love." Is that you?

MK: That is me, but I'm not naturally inclined toward the mystical.

JK: The more improbable the story, the deeper you believe?

MK: When I have this conversation with people who mock my faith, I find they have all kinds of mystical beliefs. My skeptical friend whose husband died thinks he talks to her through the wind chimes. No, not big on the improbable.

JK: You write about a "carnal" Christianity. And I think of Manet's painting at the Metropolitan Museum of Art, "Dead Christ with Angels." Seeing it was the first time I thought of Christ as real --- real enough to be a corpse.

MK: I didn't get Jesus either. I came in on the Holy Spirit, this vague force for benevolence. When I got baptized, I thought Jesus had too many barnacles. He was not a smart guy. He was unnecessarily fucked up. Then I did thirty weeks of St. Ignatius's spiritual exercises, and I got a sense of Jesus as a human unit.

JK: Toward the end of the book, you're assigned two Bible passages. You open your mother's Bible and find --- like an arrow shot across 70 years --- that she marked them both when she was a kid. And no other passages in the book are marked. You say: "I know how specifically designed we are for each other." In essence, aren't you saying that God holds us all in the palm of His hand?

MK: It's the Reinhold Niebuhr quote: "We're put on earth a little while to learn to bear the beams of love."

JK: Do you feel with this book that you have, for needy readers, ceased to be a writer and have become, like a liberal Peggy Noonan, a spiritual sob sister --- a beacon for the broken and lost?

MK: Oh, please! You don't understand what happened when "Liar's Club" came out. I had 80 page letters from death row and pre-op transsexuals. I think what we do when we read together is to enter into a community. We take suffering into the body and transform it.

JK: How are you going to talk about your belief on your tour and in interviews?

MK: Let me tell you: Talking about this to a secular audience is like doing card tricks on the radio. People will think I'm nuts. But I have to do this. And, just so you know, the people who knew me when I was drinking think I'm much improved --- they say, "I can't believe you're not crazy." And that's what I like about Catholicism: the quality of realism in this practice. Sounds crazy, but it's true. We are sinners --- we do want to eat the candy and fuck the Fedex guy and suck cocaine off each other's chests.

JK: Does faith make writing easier?

MK: Yes. It makes everything easier. Working on this book, at one point, I considered selling my apartment and giving the money back. Then I let go of the outcome. Sure, I want to sell a million copies and be on Oprah. I don't know if that's in my best interest. But I think God knows. So that relieves you of a lot of fear about the marketplace. I saw a picture of myself in the Wall Street Journal the other day. I looked like Nosferatu. I'd rather look like Cindy Crawford, but these days, I really don't sweat it.■

Caroline Knapp:
"Drinking: A Love Story"

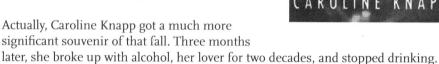

She was running across the street
with her best friend's kids on her back
when she lost her balance. Her fall was
brilliant --- she shielded the kids from
smashing their skulls. Her reward: "a
gash on the knee so deep the nurses
could see my kneecap."

Actually, Caroline Knapp got a much more
significant souvenir of that fall. Three months
later, she broke up with alcohol, her lover for two decades, and stopped drinking.

Caroline Knapp an alcoholic? No way! She grew up in Cambridge, Massachusetts,
the daughter of the department head of psychosomatic medicine at Boston University Medical School. After graduating from Brown, she became a writer, and a good
one; she wrote a popular column for The Boston Phoenix and became its lifestyle
editor. She worked out. She had relationships. In little more than a year, both her
parents died --- and she still finished a book.

If you know your drunks, you already know Caroline Knapp's breed: "high-functioning alcoholic."

But why did Caroline Knapp have her first drink at 12, her first drunk at 14? Did she
really become an alcoholic because, at 16, she felt a boyfriend slipping away and, to
bolster her self-esteem, poured a whole bottle of wine down her throat?

This book is really two stories.

One is a squalid tale: hidden bottles, overlapping romances, early morning surprises in strange beds, and, mostly, lies lies lies. But it is not a tale of paper bags
and alleys and the dry heaves. The locations are chic bars in Boston and a summer
home on Martha's Vineyard --- this is not a woman who ever slipped out for a drink
at lunch.

The other is a family history, revealed with the skill you expect from a shrink's
daughter --- or a thriller writer. Because, to the knowledge of Caroline Knapp the
alcoholic, alcohol addiction didn't run in her family. Her father had a martini or two
when he came from work at night. Her mother's connection to alcohol was mostly

to set out bowls of carrots and peanuts. So it wasn't as if she learned to drink at the feet of experts. Or did she?

In 280 mesmerizing pages, these stories merge. How could they not; they're the same story, told two ways. Along the way, Knapp takes us inside the head of the alcoholic with an exactitude that's spooky.

Caroline Knapp published "Drinking" and won a ton of praise. She replaced bad boyfriends with a dog and wrote a different kind of love story, "Pack of Two: The Intricate Bond Between People and Dogs," also much praised.

In April of 2002, Knapp --- a constant smoker --- was diagnosed with lung cancer. In May, she married her boyfriend. In June, she died. She was 42.

I could tell you the stats about the immensity of alcohol abuse in America, and how alcohol plays a part so big in domestic violence, rape and murder that we can scarcely stand to talk about it. Instead, I direct you to the Guest Book created after Caroline Knapp's death. As I write, it runs to 66 pages. Many of the messages are like this: *I started your book and I couldn't put it down, and, reading it, I realized I have a problem, and I knew I had to deal with it. And I went to the Web to find out how to thank you, only to learn that you died. How I wish I could tell you.*

If you've got a problem or if someone you love has a problem, don't wait until the cops are asking how the car could have killed that kid. But ignore my exhortations. Take it from the experts on that message board: This is the book that can make the penny drop. Especially the last few pages --- because as Caroline Knapp came to see it, there is nothing more beautiful than a roomful of strangers, drinking boiled coffee, getting through life one sober day at a time. ∎

J.R. Moehringer: "The Tender Bar"

His father was out of his mother's life before J.R. was old enough to remember that he was ever around. ("My father was a man of many talents, but his one true genius was disappearing.") His mother, suddenly poor, moves into her family's house in Manhasset, Long Island.

Also in that house: Uncle Charlie, a bartender at Dickens, a Manhasset establishment beloved by locals who appreciate liquor in quantity--- "every third drink free" --- and strong opinions, served with a twist.

A boy needs a father. If he doesn't have one, he needs some kind of man in his life. Or men, because it can indeed take a village.

You know how a book like this must work: First the heartbreak, then the healing. Early on, there's a scene that tells you how deep the wound is: J.R.'s father calls to say he's taking J.R., age 8 or so, to a Mets game. The appointed hour comes. And goes. Late that night, his mother comes home and asks about the game. And then this:

I wrapped my arms around her, startled by how much I loved her and how intensely I needed her. As I held my mother, clung to her, cried against her legs, it struck me that she was all I had, and if I didn't take good care of her I'd be lost.

To take good care of her, J.R. must become a man. But where will he find the men who will help him grow up?

He starts with Uncle Charlie. One night J.R. watches "Casablanca".... and sees his uncle as Humphrey Bogart. And although he was just eight years old, "I began to dream of going to Dickens as other boys dream of visiting Disneyland."

J.R. gets his chance when his grandfather runs out of cigarettes and he's sent to the bar to buy a pack. The air was "a beautiful pale yellow." Each breath "tasted like beer." There were "white-faced men with orange hair and red noses." And "astonishing" women.

J.R.'s a good ten years away from being legal. But Uncle Charlie starts including him in outings with the bar's inner circle. One drunken day at the beach they're stumped by a word game.

"Richard's Ingredients --- what is that?"
J.R. had the answer: "Nixon's Fixin's."
"The kid," Colt said.
"Holy shit," Bobo said.
"Give him another," Joey D said.
Uncle Charlie looked at J.R., then back at the newspaper. He read: "Terrific Gary."
J.R. said, "Super Cooper."

With that, everything changes. The men no longer treat J.R. "as a seagull that had wandered into their midst." Now they teach him: how to throw a curve, how to shrug, the importance of confidence. There is a trip to Shea Stadium so magical it more than makes up for his father's cruelty --- and at the very end of that chapter, there is a change so sudden, so dramatic, so totally sad, that you have to read it a second time, just to believe it.

The characters from the bar are --- what else? --- wonderfully engaging. Uncle Charlie, of course. A tough guy, Joey D. A Vietnam vet, Cager. Bob the Cop. Smelly. Colt. And a chorus of major drinkers. No wonder that, in time, the bar itself became J.R.'s father, "its dozens of men melding into one enormous male eye looking over my shoulder."

But it's in the high school years that "The Tender Bar" really catches fire. We're past the easy jokes now ---- "Beer: a beverage, but also a meal" --- and into experiences that resonate. The guys who turn J.R. on to books. His first time. Applying to college. Getting in. The girl friend from heaven --- and hell. Graduation. The hilarious first job, and then the real one. And, at every turn, the men of the Dickens bar: their stories, their wisdom and their folly.

I'm being vague on the facts here, and for a reason: While I desperately want you to read this book, I don't want to ruin it for you. And J.R. Moehringer is such a gifted writer --- he has a Pulitzer Prize for journalism --- that his chapters are structured like small, linked bombs. The detonations are cumulative; by the end, you're deeply immersed in half a dozen lives. And, of course, a few deaths.

But, you say, *a bar?* Moehringer provides context:

In ancient Greece, there were amphitheaters, and there was plenty of wine served at amphitheaters. There needs to be a place where people come together, freed from their possessions and temporarily free of their houses and their identities to some extent and where they can be in semidarkness and tell the old stories. This is the very place where I decided that I wanted to find a way to tell stories for a living, and it's also the place where I first saw a man give his memoir. It was at this bar where I didn't know what it was at the time but I saw a guy tell his life story. And when he was done, he felt better about his life.

It's said that time spent in a bar is, like time spent fly-fishing, time outside of life. Moehringer captures that brilliantly. In his years at the oak plank, he made many notes on paper napkins, and what he heard has served him well, for his one-liners are timeless and priceless. "Do not laugh at me, pal," a man says. "My mother laughed at me and I had her operated on needlessly." Great stuff, and there's lots more of it.

Moehringer collected these notes, and, for years, thought he could turn them into a novel. He couldn't. Then 9/11 came along. Nearly 50 people from Manhasset died in the Towers; Moehringer, who was by then working in the West, came home to write about his home town. No jokes here, just funerals, and "the kind of crying I could tell would last for years."

The man who writes about those men and women is a writer the men of Dickens would be proud of --- he's not only learned what they had to teach him, he's gone beyond. He's performed psychic surgery on himself; he's at once painfully self-aware and fully functional. He can go from lunatic to serious in a sentence. He can forgive. Many talk of "moving on," and their jaws are all that moves; this guy did it, and it shows in every sentence.

The bar is no more. The men who schooled J.R, are, by now, dead or decrepit. But they --- and his mother --- did a helluva job on this kid. And he has returned the favor with an act of love, a remembrance that picks at every scab and still delivers hope.

I couldn't put "The Tender Bar" down. ■

Jacques Sandulescu: "Donbas: A True Story of an Escape Across Russia"

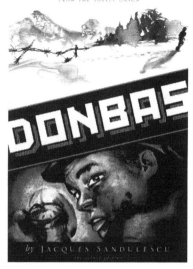

by JACQUES SANDULESCU

When I first encountered Jacques Sandulescu, I was a pasty college kid whose idea of exertion involved a highlighter and a textbook. Jacques was twice my age, a giant, rock hard, with hands that swallowed pens whole. Romania was deep in his past, as was his career as a professional boxer. In 1968, when we met, he was a Greenwich Village bar owner.

Like Big Daddy Lipscomb --- the legendary giant of a football player who used to help opponents up "so the children won't think Big Daddy's mean" --- Jacques was a calming force in every room he entered. You couldn't imagine trouble erupting with him around; he was that big and strong. And, at the same time, peaceful --- he had the kind of calm only people who have passed through fire seem to know.

It wasn't until I read his book that I understood the horror Jacques survived.

"I was arrested in Brasov on my way to school," his book begins. And right there your stomach sinks. Because you know what's coming: a terrible story, told in unadorned prose.

As "Donbas" opens, Jacques is 16 years old, 6 feet 2 inches tall, 180 pounds. He's the youngest person in the boxcar filled with Romanians that the Russians are shipping east in January of 1945. But his youth vanishes fast when he watches guards execute some would-be escapees. On one hand, he envies their death: "no more cold, misery, hunger." On the other, he wants to live. Which means he'll have to escape.

This is a book about noticing everything, paying sharp attention, looking for an opening. His first conclusion: Don't try to escape in winter, don't think you can get out of Russia without knowing Russian.

But after a few days of working in the coalmines of Donbas (now considered part of the Ukraine), his thoughts turn from escape to survival. The work is wet and cold.

A cave-in could come at any time. Exhaustion, exposure, hunger --- death comes in many forms here.

I have never read an account of work in a mine that made me so claustrophobic. I found myself reading faster, as if getting to the end of a particularly horrible shift would provide some relief. But it didn't --- above ground, there were sadistic guards and icy winds. "Many prisoners died," Jacques reports matter-of-factly. "Over half the camp. Four hundred and fifty weak and sick weren't suffering any more."

Jacques is comparatively well off. He is strong and uncomplaining, a good worker. He gets privileges --- when he goes to nearby homes for dinner, it's a delight to read as he eats and eats and eats. But he's never fooled; there's always a power-mad guard around the corner. And one does beat him so badly he almost dies. Which makes it all the more satisfying when, with the permission of a senior officer, Jacques stomps that sadist mercilessly. "It was a good feeling while it lasted," he says. I think even a pacifist would agree.

After two and a half years, his luck runs out. Jacques is trapped in a cave-in and rescued only by a friend's heroic efforts. He fears his legs will be amputated. It's winter, but so what --- he must escape. His legs are running with pus, he is a mass of sores, but he slips onto a train, hides in an open coal car and begins the slow, freezing ride to the West.

Books like this have a built-in handicap --- we know the author survived. Only the best of the breed make us forget that there's a happy ending. And this is the best; reading these pages, you will feel cold and hungry, raging with fever, wet and dispirited. But mostly, you will feel Jacques Sandulescu's spirit, his unyielding insistence on life, life in free air, life at all costs. After you put his book down, you will, literally, take a deep breath. ■

Patti Smith: "Just Kids"

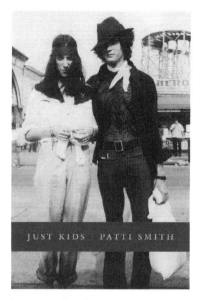

At 14, Patti was a "skinny loser," a frequent occupant of the dunce chair. She was also, God bless her, a reader, "smitten by the book." Her family was always short on money --- her mother was a waitress, her father a factory worker --- so they moved often, ending up in Camden, New Jersey.

For her 16th birthday, her mother gave her "The Fabulous Life of Diego Rivera." That summer, as she worked in a factory, inspecting handlebars for tricycles, she dreamed that she was Frida Kahlo, "both muse and maker."

Robert Mapplethorpe grew up on Long Island. He was mischievous and handsome, "tinged with a fascination for beauty." His family was neat, orderly, Catholic. They weren't talkers, they weren't readers. They were "safe."

At 20, Patti got pregnant, left school, gave up her child. She found solace in Rimbaud, in the idea of a burning passion for art. That meant New York City. She went to buy a bus ticket, discovered the fare had gone up. Then, in a phone booth, she found a handbag. There was money inside. She took it, blessing her unknown benefactor.

In New York, she slept in the park, cadged day-old bread. That was just inconvenience. What was real: "It was the summer Coltrane died." And it was the summer she met her great love and dark twin. They moved in together and dedicated themselves to art.

Robert Mapplethorpe got AIDS and died in 1989. Long before, Patti Smith had become the Poet Laureate of New York punk music. Her memoir, "Just Kids," is the winner of the National Book Award for Non-Fiction.

Who doesn't love to read about the struggling years of people who become great successes? This is among the best of that breed --- the story of a woman with a pure heart who willed herself to be an artist and a man who loved art with the same intensity but with a cool eye for the ways it could launch him into money, fame, Society. To her credit, Smith is no blinkered keeper of the flame. She acknowledges

Mapplethorpe's worldly ambitions: "We were both praying for Robert's soul, he to sell it and I to save it."

Still, the title is exactly right. "One cannot imagine the mutual happiness we felt when we sat and drew together." When they took a break, she boiled water and made Nescafé. After a good session, they splurged on Mallomars, Robert's favorite treat. They had their differences --- Robert wanted to be Warhol, Patti "hated the soup and felt little for the can" --- but it didn't matter. All that was important was mutual support, their unending belief in the other's talent. Progress was measured in the work. And in baby steps: "We now had enough money for two sandwiches."

Eventually, they make it to the Hotel Chelsea, haven for the hip and artistic. They hang out at Max's Kansas City. And now we start to recognize the names. In the Automat, Allen Ginsberg tries to pick Patti up --- he thought she was "a very pretty boy." She meets a friend of Dylan's, who brings her to meet Janis Joplin. She starts an affair with Sam Shepherd without knowing who he is.

And, finally, Robert comes to terms with his sexuality. He and Patti stop living together even as they affirm undying love. He trades drawing for photography and begins to take the gorgeous pictures of nude men and flowers that led to his first success. And then, as Smith delicately puts it, he "took areas of dark human consent and turned them into art."

The rest of the story is one you may already know. She picked up a guitar, set her poems to music, started a band. As ever, she was a crusader for art:

We imagined ourselves as the Sons of Liberty with a mission to preserve, protect, and project the revolutionary spirit of rock and roll. We feared that the music which had given us sustenance was in danger of spiritual starvation. We feared it losing its sense of purpose, we feared it falling into fattened hands, we feared it floundering in a mire of spectacle, finance, and vapid technical complexity. We would call forth in our minds the image of Paul Revere, riding through the American night, petitioning the people to wake up, to take up arms. We too would take up arms, the arms of our generation, the electric guitar and the microphone.

Dylan came to see her. Springsteen wrote "Because the Night" with her. Then she married Fred Sonic Smith --- "a king among men and men knew him" --- and moved to Detroit to start a family.

"Robert was diagnosed with AIDS at the same time I found I was carrying my second child." That is some sentence. But then, so many are --- my copy of "Just Kids" has more pencil marks in the margins than any book I've read this year. It's not just her writing, though, that grabs me. It's her spirit.

"We were as Hansel and Gretel and we ventured out into the black forest of the world." And then one was left to tell the story. It's not the whole story, and some of it strikes me as made-up as Dylan's memoir, but no matter --- I completely believe their commitment to their work. And I pray that when my daughter is, say, fourteen, she'll pick this book up and let it work its magic.■

Michael Tonello:
"Bringing Home the Birkin: My Life in Hot Pursuit of the World's Most Coveted Handbag"

Beyonce got some sweet gifts yesterday. Her husband, Jay-Z, was spotted shopping at the Hermes boutique on Christmas Eve. A spy reports, "Jay was in a private room doing last-minute shopping. He had a guard standing watch outside. He spent $350,000 on Birkin bags, among other things.
--- New York Post, 12/26/10

Jane Birkin was flying from London to Paris in 1981 when she reached into her bag for her datebook and everything fell out. "I'd love a bag with pockets," the English singer/actress told her seatmate.

Her seatmate just happened to be the chairman of Hermès. He was a good listener. He had his designers make a bag with pockets, and he sent one to Birkin ---and named it after her.

Then the fun began.

Everything at Hermès is expensive. Like: a scarf at $725. Or a leather shoulder bag at $6,500. The datebook Jane Birkin used? It now costs $1,025.

The Birkin bag, however, was in another league. Not only was it expensive, you couldn't get one. Why? Oh, because each bag required 48 hours of craftsmanship. You know: "This isn't a bag, it's a work of art."

Demand soon outstripped supply.

Well, not really. But that was the marketing line. And a genius one at that. Create a luxury item so special it doesn't need a logo. Then make it scarce. Very scarce --- at one point, Hermès announced there was a two-year waiting list. Which only made the Birkin more desirable.

It's a venerable truth: Deny the rich what they want, and they'll pay anything to get it.

It was only a matter of time --- and technology --- before Michael Tonello came along.

Our good fortune: Michael Tonello is a delightful writer, and "Bringing Home the Birkin: My Life in Hot Pursuit of the World's Most Coveted Handbag" is one of the most enjoyable books I've read in years.

Tonello's outrageous story as a Birkin buyer --- and reseller, or, as he liked to think of himself, "leather liaison" --- began with him living on Cape Cod and jetting off to exotic destinations for fashion shoots "with a can of hairspray and a powder puff." He gets an assignment in Barcelona. He falls in love with the city. And moves there.

Money, how to make it. He took one of his scarves --- purchased years earlier for $99 at Ralph Lauren --- and sold it on eBay for $430. He sold a Truman Capote first edition for $1,000. He saw the excitement on an eBay board for Hermès scarves, so he sold one of his for a $400 profit.

And then a curious thing happened --- people who didn't get to buy his scarf wrote to ask him if he had more. He went to Hermès in Barcelona, bought two dozen and sold them for a "sizable" profit. He discovered that these scarves cost $30 less at the Hermès store in Andorra, so he made the two-hour drive and bought the first of a thousand scarves he'd purchase there.

Soon he was selling 30 scarves a week.

All because he saw a niche in the market.

All because Hermès didn't yet have a web site.

Inevitably, one of his customers --- who just happened to be songwriter Carole Bayer Sager --- asked if he could get her a Birkin. He had no idea what that was, but once he found out, he was a bag-seeking missile.

How Michael Tonello cracked the code and was able to buy Birkins from Hermès is the centerpiece of the book. It is hilarious --- if, that is, you are amused by the foibles of the rich and those who cater to them. It is tender --- if, that is, you can be touched by Tonello's burgeoning friendships with the women who became his best customers. It is even thrilling --- if, that is, your heart rate jumps when a French colleague tries to rip Tonello off and Tonello must Take Steps.

Now? No more waiting list. And now that anybody can buy a Birkin, anyone can sell one. Like Amazon, which has offered a knockoff for just $44.99, with free shipping.

So much for "special."

What's special is this book. ■

BOOKS

MYSTERY

Raymond Chandler: "The Big Sleep"

Raymond Chandler cut his typing paper in half. He'd type until he made a bad word choice or botched a bit of dialogue, then he'd rip the sheet out of his typewriter and start again. Eventually he'd have a half page of fiction he could stand. Then he'd move on to the next half-page of his novel.

Only slaves to perfection work like this. But if you're brilliant --- and in the late 1930s, Chandler was inventing a new kind of hero and a new way of writing detective fiction --- you get "The Big Sleep." It was Chandler's first novel, but any lover of crime fiction will tell you: This is a masterpiece and then some.

If you stay up late or are an aficionado of old movies, you have seen the Howard Hawks film. It stars Humphrey Bogart and Lauren Bacall. It co-stars Los Angeles in the rain, shady supper clubs, a pornography business masquerading as a rare bookstore, and a host of minor characters --- almost all of them memorable, even when you can't keep them straight. And if you can't keep the characters straight, don't worry --- Chandler couldn't either. There are seven murders in this twisted tale, and even he was unsure who committed one of them.

One of the screenwriters was William Faulkner. He most notably contributed a memorably smutty exchange between Bogart and Bacall, but his work was not onerous --- most of the snappy dialogue in the film comes directly from the book. But what was added in the movie is less interesting than what was, by necessity, lost in the transition from book to film: Chandler's prose.

The story starts simply enough. General Sternwood, the aged and ill father of two wild daughters, has summoned a private investigator. Philip Marlowe --- a former cop, at once brutally cynical and totally incorruptible --- narrates the book. And in the first paragraph, we learn most of what we need to know about him: "I was neat, clean, shaved and sober, and I didn't care who knew it. I was everything the well-dressed private detective ought to be."

General Sternwood has a small piece of business for Marlowe: paying off a rare-book dealer who seems to have accumulated several thousand dollars of his younger daughter's gambling debts. But one thing leads to another, and soon we are in a world of drugs and smut and a great deal of police indifference. And it is here that Chandler simply leaves lesser writers behind --- he strips away all our pretty illusions about the ways tough guys behave. In essence, he turns every character into an extreme, movie version of himself/herself. Consider:

"How come you had a key?"
"Is that any of your business, soldier?"
"I could make it my business."
He smiled tightly and pushed his hat back on his gray hair. "And I could make your business my business."
"You wouldn't like it. The pay's too small."

And then there are the lines that make you reach for a pencil. My favorites:

"Dead men are heavier than broken hearts."

"She brought the glass over. Bubbles rose in it like false hopes."

"The Big Sleep" --- the title is a euphemism for death --- races through five days and nights. You can read it in one. You will likely come away with a great admiration for Raymond Chandler and an interest in reading more of his novels. But be warned: You may also set the book down with a revised --- that is, lesser --- appreciation of a batch of mystery writers who once thrilled you. ■

Dashiell Hammett:
"The Glass Key"

"The Glass Key," published in 1930, was Dashiell Hammett's favorite book --- quite a statement when you consider that he also wrote "The Thin Man" and "The Maltese Falcon."

"The clues were nicely placed there," he explained, "although nobody seemed to see them."

He's right. "The Glass Key" is a cleverly plotted novel, with more than its share of plot twists and turns. It's got a love triangle of sorts (and even a risqué scene that will fuel a fantasy some cold night). And in its style, it's quite innovative: We're never told what the characters think. Instead, we have to figure out their motivations from their actions --- and in addition to the expected sharp dialogue, there's plenty of rough-and-tumble action in these 214 pages.

But I don't think that's why readers respond to this book.

It's the politics.

In "The Glass Key," we see what political corruption looks like --- from the inside.

Ned Beaumont describes himself as "a gambler and a politician's hanger-on." That's too modest. He does most of the smart thinking for Paul Madvig, a behind-the-scenes power broker who controls large chunks of an unnamed city. Ned is no bruiser --- he's tall, tubercular and a sucker for a stiff drink --- but on occasion he's Madvig's enforcer.

And there is much to enforce: a creep named Shad O'Rory is hoping his candidates will control the city after the upcoming election. Then there is the small matter of a Senator's son, found dead in the street, right in the middle of Chapter One.

Everyone has an angle. The Senator needs Paul Madvig's support. Madvig wants to marry the Senator's daughter. Madvig's daughter was having an affair with the Senator's son. And Madvig looks like the boy's most likely killer. (Got all that? It's simpler in the movie.)

Beaumont persuades the District Attorney to give him limited authority to investigate the case. His aim, of course, is to slow that investigation down. Which he does by planting a key piece of evidence.

And that's not half of it. The newspaper publisher is heavily in debt. The mortgage on his plant is held by a bank that favors a candidate not in Madvig's stable. So what? As Beaumont points out, "He'll do what he's told to do and print what he's told to print."

Dirty stuff, all of it. Which isn't to say there's no hero. There is: Ned Beaumont. How can that be? Because there's a thin vein of idealism in Ned. Because he has a code. Because, in the end, he is a gentleman. And because he recognizes that Madvig, though corrupt, has the city's interests at heart.

That's what makes "The Glass Key" so fascinating --- the way it presents a raw, ugly reality and then makes a kind of sense of it. Is moral order restored at the end? The title tells us it can't be; the glass key is a phrase from a young woman's dream. Yes, it can open a door. Once. Then it shatters. And the door can never be locked again. You don't need deep Freudian understanding to grasp that he's talking about the price of worldly knowledge --- that is, the end of innocence.

In "The Glass Key," men are always smoking dappled cigars. Some of them wear both vests and hats. They make corruption almost stylish. ■

Jim Thompson:
"The Killer Inside Me"

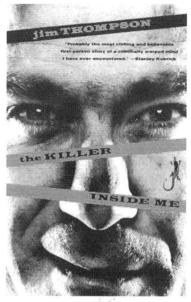

The first time I read it I wasn't right for days. This is not an uncommon experience. The novel is narrated by the main character, Lou Ford, deputy sheriff of Central City, Texas (population: 48,000). His is a twisted tale, told by a sociopath from his point of view.

How twisted? This book leaves "Silence of the Lambs" in the dust. Blame it on the sex --- the violent sex and the violence after sex. Hannibal Lecter may kill, but he's cool and scientific about it, and because "Silence" has a third-person narrator with some restraint, we don't see him eating someone's liver and fava beans as he drinks a nice Chianti.

But because Lou Ford is our tour guide, we see his murders from inches away. Relatively speaking, it's no big deal when he kills a man. It's what Lou does to women that's truly sickening: overwhelming them, beating them, punishing them, humiliating them. We're chained to his point-of-view, so his sick, violent misogyny involves and implicates us. And, possibly, worse: turns us on in sick places we never knew we had.

Critics sometimes defend books like this on the grounds that they are "moral" tales. And the novel does scream that Lou Ford isn't just sick, he's evil. Stanley Kubrick, a film director who knew a thing or three about evil, called this "probably the most chilling and believable first-person story of a criminally warped mind I have ever encountered." That's because Jim Thompson, who also wrote "The Grifters" and "The Getaway," had no problem looking into the darkest reaches of the human soul and mirthlessly presenting what he found --- that is, violence, corruption and nihilism.

Thompson knocked off "The Killer Inside Me" in just four weeks. Published in 1952, it was a shocker, and not just because of the violence and the sex. Even on a good day, Lou Ford is disturbing. He's the kind of dullard you do anything to avoid --- he spouts the most inane cliché, he's Mr. Hearty to one and all, he's so damn friendly and boring he drives everybody crazy.

What nobody gets: He's really a kind of genius who acts like a dope on purpose. All to keep them from guessing that, when no one is looking, he's a serial killer who's kinky as hell.

And then there's the writing, which is as blunt as the brutality it describes.
Like this:

She still didn't get it. She laughed, frowning a little at the same time.
"But Lou --- that doesn't make sense. How could I be dead when...?'
"Easy," I said. And I gave her a slap. And still she didn't get it.
She put a hand to her hand to her face and rubbed it slowly.
"Y-you'd better not do that, now, Lou. I've got to travel, and --"
"You're not going anywhere, baby," I said, and I hit her again.
And then she got it.

Why read such horrifying, disgusting stuff? Precisely because it's so acutely ren-
dered --- no writer creates psychopaths more compelling than Jim Thompson. And
no writer I can think of can put you inside a sicko's head as totally as Thompson.
You may not like what he has to say, but you have to admire his ability to say it.

This book gives new definition to the phrase "guilty pleasure." Just make sure you
don't have to be anywhere after you start reading it --- if you don't put it down out of
squeamishness, you're not going to be able to tear yourself away from "The Killer
Inside Me." ∎

BOOKS

Cooking

Julia Child and Simone Beck: "Mastering The Art of French Cooking, Volume One"

The movie "Julie & Julia" is built around the astonishing idea that a fan of "Mastering The Art of French Cooking, Volume One" would cook her way through the book's almost 600 recipes in a single year. I've been using this book for three decades and I've only made a fraction of the recipes. But I've made that fraction so many times that the pages fall open to my favorite recipes.

The other way to identify my favorites? Greasy pages. Makes sense. As Child gaily told her television audience, "If you're afraid of butter, as many people are nowadays, just put in cream!"

Such bluntness was her nature --- and her charm. She came from money and privilege; the challenge of her life was to find something worth committing herself to. First came Paul Child. Then, at 37, came the Cordon Bleu cooking school in Paris. And then, through a bit of luck, came an opportunity to work with Simone Beck on a French cookbook for Americans. As she tells the story in "My Life in France," that book took almost a decade.

Judith Jones was the first American editor to read the manuscript. She flipped:

I pored over the recipe for a beef stew and learned the right cuts of meat for braising, the correct fat to use (one that would not burn), the importance of drying the meat and browning it in batches, the secret of the herb bouquet, the value of sautéing the garnish of onions and mushrooms separately. I ran home to make the recipe --- and my first bite told me that I had finally produced an authentic French boeuf bourguignon --- as good as one I could get in Paris. This, I was convinced, was a revolutionary cookbook, and if I was so smitten, certainly others would be.

Quality mattered. So did timing. "Mastering The Art of French Cooking, Volume One" was published in 1961. In the White House was a President with a wife who loved France. Air travel was replacing ocean liners --- Americans in larger numbers were traveling to Europe. Frozen food and TV dinners were clogging the supermarmarkets; Child lobbied for accessible sophistication and changed the way some of us ate.

And then there was multi-media. WGBH, Boston's public TV station, invited Child to promote her book. The station had no studio kitchen, so she brought eggs, a whisk and a hot plate. On camera, she made an omelet, narrating the process with wit and confidence. A TV series soon followed --- she was Martha Stewart before there was Martha Stewart.

Actually, she was much more. Back then, cooking was not a respected profession. She showed that it was a discipline --- and an art. And she legitimized the home-gourmet. Was cooking a chore? Not after you'd seen Julia Child amusing herself as she prepared dinner.

All these years later, I'm still charmed by Child's 13-page screed on omelets. On the other hand, I never had much use for her pâtés or terrines, soufflés or sauces. Dessert still seems like overkill. And the seven recipes for kidney? Non-events. It's the classics that first appealed to me, and still do. I share two of those recipes here. If you'll try them, you'll raise a glass to Child and Beck --- and, like me, you'll soon have a food-smeared cookbook on your shelves.

Vichyssoise
Serves 6 to 8

3 cups sliced leeks, white part only
3 cups sliced potatoes, old or baking potatoes recommended
1 and 1/2 quarts of chicken stock or canned chicken broth
1 to 2 teaspoons salt or to taste
1/2 to 1 cup heavy cream
 2 to 3 tablespoons minced fresh chives

Simmer the leeks and potatoes in the broth, covering partially, for 20 to 30 minutes, until the vegetables are tender. Puree the soup in a blender or food mill. Stir in the cream. Season to taste oversalting slightly as salt loses flavor in a cold dish. Chill. Serve in chilled soup cups.

Coq au Vin
Serves 4

4 ounce chunk of bacon
20 pearl onions, peeled, or 1 large yellow onion, sliced
1 chicken, 4 lb, cut into serving pieces, or 3 lbs chicken parts, excess fat trimmed, skin on
2 garlic cloves, peeled and mashed
Salt and pepper to taste

2 cups chicken stock
3 cups young, full-bodied red wine
1 bay leaf
Several fresh thyme sprigs
Several fresh parsley sprigs
1/2 lb button mushrooms, trimmed and roughly chopped
2 Tablespoons butter
1/2 Tablespoon tomato paste

Blanch the bacon to remove some of its saltiness. Drop the bacon into a saucepan of cold water, covered by a couple of inches. Bring to a boil, simmer for 5 minutes, drain. Rinse in cold water, pat dry with paper towels. Cut the bacon into 1 inch by 1/4 inch pieces.

Brown bacon on medium high heat in a dutch oven big enough to hold the chicken, about 5 minutes. Remove the cooked bacon, set aside. Keep the bacon fat in the pan. Add onions and chicken, skin side down. Brown the chicken well, on all sides, about 10 minutes.

Halfway through the browning, add the garlic and sprinkle the chicken with salt and pepper. (Note: it is best to add salt while cooking, not just at the very end. It brings out the flavor of the chicken.)

Spoon off any excess fat. Add the chicken stock, wine, and herbs. Add back the bacon. Lower heat to a simmer. Cover and cook for 20-30 minutes, or until chicken is tender and cooked through. Remove chicken and onions to a separate platter. Remove the bay leaves, herb sprigs, garlic, and discard.

Add mushrooms to the remaining liquid and turn the heat to high. Boil quickly and reduce the liquid by three fourths until it becomes thick and saucy. Lower the heat, stir in the butter. Return the chicken and onions to the pan to reheat and coat with sauce. Adjust seasoning. Garnish with parsley and serve. ■

Marcella Hazan:
"Essentials of Classic
Italian Cooking"

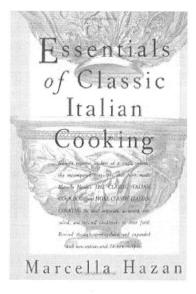

Until Marcella Hazan published her cookbook, you went to a restaurant that featured decent Italian cooking, had a meal destined for your top ten list, and returned home with a nagging question: This is "simple" food. Why can't I cook like this?

With Hazan's book in hand, that changed. Her recipes were the essence of simplicity --- her famous tomato sauce contained only tomatoes, onion, butter and salt. But not so fast. As she pointed out: "Simple doesn't mean easy." Her definition of "simple" was not for the lazy: "I can describe simple cooking thus: Cooking that is stripped all the way down to those procedures and those ingredients indispensable in enunciating the sincere flavor intentions of a dish."

So she began her book by setting forth some fundamentals.

Turn to page seven. "Flavor, in Italian dishes, builds up from the bottom," she begins. "It is not a cover, it is a base. In a pasta sauce, a *risotto*, a fricassee, a stew, or a dish of vegetables, a foundation of flavor supports, lifts, points up the principal ingredients." The metaphor, she continues, is "architectural." And you suddenly flash back to your childhood and your afternoons playing with blocks, and a very big light bulb goes on.

The light bulb here involves techniques: *battuto* (chopped vegetables), *soffritto* (sauteeing the battuto) and *insaporire* (bestowing taste, by coating the key ingredients with the flavoring elements). Her explanation is clear. By page nine, you are ready to cook.

Marcella's "secret" might just be the result of her fundamental innocence. She said she never cooked until her marriage in 1955. Her training was in science --- she had a PhD in biology from the University of Ferrara, Italy. Which explains her heightened sensitivity to fundamentals --- to process.

Just look at the recipes in these 704 pages. Few have more than 10 ingredients. Instructions put you in charge (you observe the meal you're cooking, you decide when it's done). And she makes sure that you won't be standing in the kitchen putting on the "finishing touches" while your guests twiddle their thumbs at the table --- this is hearty, traditional, Northern Italian "home cooking" that you can master for considerably less than the $3,000 that Hazan used to charge for a week of cooking classes in Venice.

You should try before you buy. In the case of a cookbook, that's easy. I let the book fall open to a recipe for a dish I make often (in part because it's terrific, but in larger part because it's incredibly easy). Here you go: a main course that is both simple and elegant, suitable for family dining and for your snootiest friends. Like the author, this recipe --- indeed, all her recipes --- is immortal.

Roast Pork with Vinegar and Bay Leaves
For 6 servings

2 tablespoons butter
1 tablespoon vegetable oil
2 pounds boneless pork loin roast
l teaspoon whole black peppercorns
salt
3 bay leaves
1/2 cup good red wine vinegar

In a heavy-bottomed or enameled cast-iron pot, put in butter and oil. Turn stove on to medium-high; when the butter foam subsides, put in the pork. Brown deeply, turning when each side is done.

Add salt, peppercorns, bay leaves and vinegar. Turn heat to low, cover the pot and cook, turning the meat occasionally. If liquid evaporates, add 1/2 cup water.

When cooked through --- 40-60 minutes --- transfer the pork to a cutting board. Let sit for a few minutes, then slice.

Meanwhile, remove bay leaves, add 2 tablespoons of water, and heat the gravy. Pour over the pork and serve.

Or try her on a recipe you've made your own way --- or someone else's --- a million times.

Bolognese Meat Sauce
for about 6 servings

1 tablespoon vegetable oil
3 tablespoons butter plus
1 tablespoon for tossing with the pasta
1/2 cup chopped onion
2/3 cup chopped celery

2/3 cup chopped carrot
3/4 pound ground beef chuck, not too lean
salt & freshly ground black pepper
1 cup whole milk [or 2 %]
Whole nutmeg for grating
1 cup dry white or red wine
1 1/2 cups canned imported Italian plum tomatoes, cut up, with their juice
1 1/4 to 1 1/2 pounds pasta
Freshly grated parmigiano-reggiano at the table

Put the oil, butter, and chopped onion in a heavy-bottomed pot and turn the heat to medium. Cook and stir until the onion is translucent. Add the celery and carrot and cook for about 2 minutes, stirring to coat the vegetables with fat.

Add the meat, a large pinch of salt, and some freshly ground pepper. Break the meat up with a fork, stir well, and cook until the meat has lost its raw color.

Add milk and let simmer gently, stirring frequently, until it has bubbled away completely. Add a tiny grating, about 1/8 teaspoon, fresh nutmeg and stir.
Add the wine and let it simmer away.

When the wine has evaporated, stir in the tomatoes. When they begin to bubble, turn the heat down so that the sauce cooks at the laziest of simmers, with just an intermittent bubble breaking through to the surface.

Cook, uncovered, for 3 hours, stirring from time to time. If the sauce begins to dry out, add 1/2 cup of water whenever necessary to keep it from sticking. At the end, there should be no water left, and the fat must separate from the sauce. Taste for salt.

Toss with cooked, drained pasta and the remaining tablespoon of butter. Serve freshly grated cheese at the table. ∎

Patricia Wells:
"Bistro Cooking"

In the fall of 1926, a 23-year-old American named A.J. Liebling sailed to France for a year of post-graduate dining. But he was not happy. The days were flying by, and he was too broke to indulge his restaurant habit at the level of his dreams.

These days, almost anyone who travels to France bearing American dollars knows how Liebling felt. If you go to Paris now, you'll find yourself in the era of the $7 café crème. So we cook French at home --- meals you'd find in a Mom-and-Pop bistro.

Patricia Wells, bless her, focused on bistros long before the economy made them chic. But then, she is one of the world's most sensible food writers; she reports on trends, but doesn't succumb to them. The French noticed her talent long ago --- she's the only woman (and the only foreigner) ever to review restaurants for a French publication.

"Bistro Cooking," published in 1989, was named Cookbook of the Year by USA Today. Good choice. The recipes are straightforward, the ingredients basic, the instructions clear. She's strong on vegetables and salads. There are half a dozen chicken entrees that can be prepared in a matter of minutes.

What recipe to choose? One of many one-dish meals that are idiot proof. It's certainly "simple" and "satisfying" --- I have served this for many Sunday lunches, and it has always required shockingly modest effort and garnered outrageous praise. The trick: The pan is lined with sliced potatoes, onions and tomatoes. The lamb is set on a rack over the vegetables. The result? As it roasts, "the lamb's wonderful juices drip into the gratin." Wells suggests that you serve this with a "solid" red wine: a Cotes-du-Rhone or Chateauneuf-du-Pape, but any Bordeaux or California Cabernet would be just as good.

Gigot Roti au Gratin de Monsieur Henry
(Roast Lamb with Monsieur Henry's Potato, Onion and Tomato Gratin)
serves 8-10

6 garlic cloves (1 clove peeled and split, the rest peeled and chopped)
1 pounds baking potatoes, peeled and sliced very thin

2 large onions, peeled and sliced very thin
5 medium tomatoes, cored and sliced very thin
1 leg of lamb, bone-in (6-7 pounds)
2/3 cup white wine
1/3 cup extra virgin olive oil
1 tablespoon fresh thyme salt, pepper

Preheat oven to 400 degrees.

Rub the bottom of a large (16 x 10 x 2) oval porcelain gratin dish (or casserole dish) with the split clove of garlic.

Arrange the potatoes in a single layer, season with salt, pepper, some of the thyme and some of the chopped garlic.

Layer the sliced onions on top, season as you did the potatoes.

Layer the tomatoes on top of the onions. Season with salt, pepper, the rest of the thyme and chopped garlic.

Pour on the white wine, then the olive oil.

Trim the thicker portions of fat from the lamb, season with salt and pepper. Set a cake or oven rack on (or in) the gratin dish and set the lamb on the rack so its juices will drip into the gratin.

Roast, uncovered, for 1 hour and 15 minutes for rare lamb (for medium lamb, roast for 15-30 more minutes). Turn the lamb every 15 minutes, basting with liquid from the gratin dish.

Remove the pan from oven and let the lamb sit for 15 minutes before carving.

Serve the thinly sliced lamb on warmed dinner plates, with the gratin alongside. Vegetable suggestion: Green or French beans.■

BOOKS

CHILDREN

Clive Barker:
"The Thief of Always"

"I never get scared by books," the child said, "but this is *really* scaring me."

For our daughter, there's no higher praise. And she sets the bar high. In her idea of a good movie, we joke, at least 1,500 people die.

What freaked her out about "The Thief of Always," and in the best possible way? The scene in which 10-year-old Harvey Swick puts on a bat's costume on Halloween night, flies high above Holiday House and has the uneasy feeling that there's a bit of vampire in his soul.

Not a feeling you usually find in fiction for kids.

That's because "The Thief of Always" was written by Clive Barker, the English jack-of-all-trades who is, by turns, an artist, novelist and the writer-director of such horror/sci-fi films as "Hellraiser" and "Candyman." The common element in his writing: what he calls "dark fantasy," in which good and evil are blended to terrifying effect.

Too tough for kids?

I'm not the only one to say it: *There's almost no book more satisfying for a 9-to-11-year-old kid to read aloud with a parent.*

That's because Clive Barker has written a story that works on two levels. One is an adventure story for kids, with a simple moral: careful what you wish for. For adults, the moral is more complex, more philosophical. For both audiences, the thrills come not only from the non-stop action but from the pared-down language.

Barker is very smart about this:

In creating 'The Thief of Always,' the vocabulary had to be simple. The structure of the sentences also had to be of a plainer style because I wanted ten-year-olds to be able to read it, but I also wanted to appeal to 40-year-olds in the same way that C.S.Lewis still appeals to me today.

And I remember as a little child I did not enjoy long descriptive passages in a novel. I liked reading a lot of action. And so when I write for children I try to keep in mind the memory of what the 10-year-old Clive Barker liked. I think the 10-year-old Clive Barker would have liked "Thief of Always."

Here's the kid version: Harvey Swick, age 10, is bored. The book starts with that:

The great grey beast February had eaten Harvey Swick alive. Here he was, buried in the belly of that smothering month, wondering if he would ever find his way out through the cold coils that lay between here and Easter.

A knock at his window, an invitation to visit a child's paradise, and Harvey willingly goes with his strange visitor to Holiday House. Magic? Try this: every morning is Spring, ever afternoon is Summer, it's Halloween every evening and Christmas every night. Glorious food. No school. Heaven on earth.

Just one catch, which, of course, the children realize too late — you can't leave.

Well, there's another. The vampire who created this place doesn't want blood. He collects souls. And he's always on the lookout for new ones, because ... but that's for you to find out. Just as your voice may shake when you get to the end and you realize what Harvey must do not just to escape Holiday House but to return their souls to who-knows-how-many children.

This book comes with a lovely publishing story. When he wrote "Thief of Always," Barker was well known as a frightmaster. He'd never written a book for kids. So....

I gave it to HarperCollins and said, 'I realize you're taking a huge risk with this, because here's a children's book coming from Clive Barker, and maybe nobody will buy it! So I'll sell it to you for a dollar.' Actually, they ended up giving me a silver dollar for it. And I did the illustrations and the thing went from there. It has since turned out to be a very successful book. It's in a lot of languages around the world and it's being taught in a lot of schools now, which is fun. I think we're at 1.5 million copies in print in America, so it wasn't bad for a book that cost them a dollar...

Millions sold. Taught in schools. Recommended by our daughter. And thoroughly enjoyed, night after night, by her aged parent as we read it aloud together. ∎

Roald Dahl

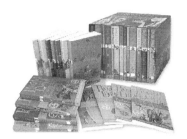

Roald Dahl is firmly on the side of children. "Parents and schoolteachers are the enemy," Dahl said. "The adult is the enemy of the child because of the awful process of civilizing this thing that when it is born is an animal with no manners, no moral sense at all."

That's his polite answer. In book after book, the message is nastier --- adults are mean and stupid, and kids must learn to defeat then.

Dahl was a genius. And a self-promoter. And, for his publishers, an abusive jerk. Another way of saying all that is that Dahl was one of those artists who was a kid all his life --- a wild child --- and that his heroes are very much like him.

This is especially the case with Willie Wonka, the candy king in "Charlie and the Chocolate Factory." Willie is a theatrical character: a showman, a circus ringleader. So was Roald Dahl --- he commanded your attention, he made your visit into an event. From earliest childhood, he loved stories and told them expertly. He adored chocolate, and had the good fortune of participating in blind tastings at a candy bar company. In his early 20s, at one of his early jobs, he began a lifelong habit: eating a candy bar after lunch. He used the silver wrappers to make a ball, which grew larger and larger. Later, he kept packets of candy in the glove compartment of his car, and gave those sweets to his kids for telling the best story on car trips.

The story of "Charlie and the Chocolate Factory" deals with the two sides of Dahl's personality --- the paranoid genius who has been stripped of his innocence by greedy and evil competitors, and the pure young boy who is heartbreaking in his goodness. As a plot device, it works out this way: Willie Wonka has closed his factory because some of his employees were selling his secrets to rival candymakers. Years pass, and he's back in business, using tiny creatures and squirrels as workers. He decides to insert five Golden Tickets in his chocolate bars. The children who find them will win a tour of the factory, with one getting a special surprise.

All the kids but Charlie Bucket are dreadful: selfish, boorish, on the make. (Their parents are overwhelmed enablers or immoral accomplices. Very satisfying.) These louts prove that Dahl is more than a kids vs. adults moralist. His kids are also cruel and loutish to other kids. Which is a delightful irony: In these stories, obnoxious kids read about obnoxious characters --- though they probably never see themselves in those characters.

"Charlie and the Chocolate Factory" was an instant hit when it was published in America in 1964; its first printing sold out in a month. In the early 1970s, Dahl produced a sequel, "Charlie and the Great Glass Elevator." Later, a movie with Gene Wilder --- a very different movie from Tim Burton's --- turned Charlie into a kids' classic.

Starting around age 8 or 9, all the smart kids I've known have loved Dahl's books, especially the ones in this collection: the two "Charlies," "James and the Giant Peach" and "The Fantastic Mr. Fox." (They have gone on, without exception, to devour more Dahl books, especially "Matilda" and "The BFG" and the memoir, "Boy.") If you have not seen them before, the drawings by Quentin Blake in these four books are superb.

Dahl's books are comedies, but they deal with the big issues: evil, integrity, loneliness. No wonder kids love them, and cherish them, and identify with their heroes. And how right it is that this flawed man produced such flawless books, one after another, the quality never faltering. ■

Shel Silverstein

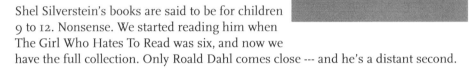

When "Every Thing On It" arrived, homework was instantly abandoned. The Girl Who Hates To Read simply had to dive into this collection of 139 poems. This speaks volumes.

Shel Silverstein's books are said to be for children 9 to 12. Nonsense. We started reading him when The Girl Who Hates To Read was six, and now we have the full collection. Only Roald Dahl comes close --- and he's a distant second.

What is Silverstein's appeal?

Simple: He's not full of the mealy-mouth bullshit that used to fill children's books. Starting way back in the '60s --- when "Ozzie and Harriet" values were finally starting to wither and die everywhere but in kids' books --- he talked to kids with respect. He thought they were smart. And creative. And they needed to be encouraged, not sedated.

Here's Silverstein's message in 34 words:

Listen to the mustn'ts, child. Listen to the don'ts. Listen to the shouldn'ts, the impossibles, the won'ts. Listen to the never haves, then listen close to me... Anything can happen, child. Anything can be.

In "Every Thing On It," he goes much further. There are poems about garlic breath and hats, but there is also this, right at the start:

Although I cannot see your face/ as you flip these poems awhile/ Somewhere from some far-off place/ I hear you laughing --- and I smile.

Wow, death! Once said to be an idea terrifying to kids. Here, addressed directly. No wonder kids love him.

Silverstein had no experience with children's books when he published his first, "Lafcadio, The Lion Who Shot Back," in 1963.

The following year, he brought out "The Giving Tree." Within the publishing world, opinion was divided. One editor said it was "too sad" and "a book for adults." Another was more direct: "That tree is sick! Neurotic!"

I loathe "The Giving Tree." Silverstein casts it as a love story --- "Once there was a tree, and she loved a little boy" --- but I see it as a study of masochism. Consider: A boy plays in a tree. As a young man, he takes some of its wood to build a house. Later, he uses more of its wood to build a book. And when he is old, and the tree is just a stump, he sits on it to rest. "And the tree was happy."

Here's my take: The tree gives and gives, with no thought to itself --- like a mother who will do anything for her beloved. I think immediately of the Mel Brooks-Carl Reiner routine in which, thousands of years ago, some parents come to visit their son in his cave. It's raining. But they don't come in --- they're happy standing in the rain and looking in. Sick! Neurotic!

But what do I know? "The Giving Tree" has sold more than 5 million copies and is the favorite book of many.

In 1974, Silverstein published "Where the Sidewalk Ends," his first collection of poems. Instant classic! Almost five million copies have been sold --- it's the all-time leader in its category.

And then came a cascade. "The Missing Piece." "A Light in the Attic" was a New York Times bestseller for 182 weeks. "Falling Up." And "Runny Babbit: A Billy Sook," a favorite in our clan. See why: "So if you say, 'Let's bead a rook/That's billy as can se,'/You're talkin' Runny Babbit talk,/Just like mim and he."

Silverstein was a ferocious worker. He wrote more than 100 one-act plays. And a batch of hit songs. But it's the books that stand above his other work. Even now, when much more is permitted, they still push the single most important idea we can present to our kids.

There is a voice inside of you
That whispers all day long,
"I feel this is right for me,
I know that this is wrong."
No teacher, preacher, parent, friend
Or wise man can decide
What's right for you --- just listen to
The voice that speaks inside. ∎

WILLIAM STEIG

"Shrek" --- yes, William Steig wrote and illustrated the book that led to the movie that became the marketing. But let's set that mega-hit aside, please, so we can look at the artist who, time after time, created books for kids that adults honestly love to read.

William Steig was the son of a house painter and a seamstress. His parents were Polish-Jewish immigrants; inevitably, they migrated to the Bronx. When the Depression battered them, their 23-year-old son Bill was the family's financial hope.

But there was a problem. "My father was a socialist --- an advanced thinker --- and he felt that business was degrading, but he didn't want his children to be laborers," Steig recalled. "We were all encouraged to go into music or art."

Well, he'd had art training. And he did like drawing. So William Steig sent a cartoon to The New Yorker in 1930 --- a picture of a prison inmate telling another, "My son's incorrigible, I can't do a thing with him." It sold. "I earned $4,500 the first year, and it was more than our family, then four of us, needed," he said.

Later, he put his early success in more Steigian terms: "I flew from the nest with my parents on my back."

Steig would become the magazine's most prolific, longest-running contributor. In 67 years --- he died, at 95, in 2003 --- he published more than 1,600 drawings and 117 New Yorker covers. It takes a dozen books to collect his cartoons.

That art is major. Steig invented a kind of free-form psychological style that has steeped into the craft so completely no one can recall a time when cartoons were just stark realism. W. H. Auden compared his drawings to Goya's "Disasters of War."

But Steig did more.

Greeting cards. He claims to have re-invented them: "They used to be all sweetness and love. I started doing the complete reverse --- almost a hate card --- and it caught on."

And then, in 1968, when he was 61, Steig started to write and illustrate children's books.

They're not like other books for kids, and that's not because of their style --- Steig didn't think about people as others did. He believed:

"People are basically good and beautiful, and neurosis is the biggest obstacle to peace and happiness."

"I'm sure we know almost nothing about what a natural child would be if there were one. But I do know that we have a lot of cute, handed-down ideas about what is good for kids. Our healthy childhood lasts only so long as it takes to destroy it, and the memory of it is buried."

"The child is the hope of humanity. If they are going to change the world, they have to start off optimistically. I wouldn't consider writing a depressing book for children."

Put those views together, and you get books that treat kids as smart and aware and verbal --- and fully capable of asking the grownups if they don't know the words. And not just any big words. I mean lunatic, sinuous, palsied, sequestration, ensconced, cloaca and cleave. Stranded on a beach, a Steigian whale is "breaded with sand." A fox feels "shabby" for his evil dreams. Like that.

Originality? "CDB!" has given generations of pre-schoolers a book they can "read" --- like this:

R U C-P?
S, I M.
I M 2.

And the stories! In "Sylvester and the Magic Pebble," a frightened donkey turns himself into a stone, but can't reverse the process. In "Dr. De Soto," a mouse that is an excellent animal dentist takes a huge chance and accepts a fox as a patient. In "The Real Thief," a goose is false accused of stealing a royal ruby.

But even more, the moral and ethical sophistication in Steig's books astonish me.

In "Amos & Boris," a mouse falls off his boat and contemplates death in terms never before seen in a kids' book: "He began to wonder what it would be like to drown. Would it take very long? Would it feel just awful? Would his soul go to heaven? Would there be other mice there?"

And the thing about Shrek isn't that he's a really gross ogre, it's the completely unexpected --- but totally Steigian --- moment when Shrek has a nightmare that he's being kissed by happy kids in a lovely field: "Some of the children kept hugging and kissing him, and there was nothing he could do to make them stop."

His favorite book, "The Real Thief," ends with this zinger: "There was peace and harmony in the kingdom once again, except for the little troubles that come up every so often even in the best of circumstances, since nothing is perfect."

Over and over, I find just the sort of affirmation I hope for in kids' books (hell, in all books). Nature heals. Friends matter. The family is a warm blanket. And quests are worth taking. And life isn't simple or easy.

Steig began a book with a quotation from William Blake:

The Angel that presided o'er my birth
Said, "Little Creature, formed of Joy and Mirth,
Go love without the help of any Thing on Earth."

I can see how Steig might feel that way; I can see how we all do. But then there are these books. They are Joy and Mirth, and they overflow with love and creativity, and any parent who has ever read them at bedtime will tell you --- they do more than help.■

John Tunis:
"The Kid from Tomkinsville"

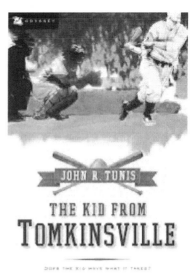

THE KID FROM
TOMKINSVILLE

The baseball novels of John R. Tunis are not only the best sports fiction for 10-to-14 year-olds ever written, they are among the best sports fiction --- period.

I should know. At age 8, I read my first Tunis novel. By age 10, I'd read them all. In my 20s, I revisited my childhood favorite --- the first book in the series, "The Kid from Tomkinsville" --- and found it held up admirably. I recently read it again. Loved it all over again.

John R. Tunis (1889-1975) was, in his time, the leading writer of teen sports stories. He had the credentials: in the late 1920s, he covered sports for a New York newspaper, then moved on to cover tennis for NBC. And then he moved into fiction, starting with "The Kid from Tomkinsville," published in 1940.

The Kid is Roy Tucker, a pitcher from a little town in Connecticut. He's working at MacKenzie's drug store "on the corner of South Main" and pitching local ball when a scout from the Brooklyn Dodgers shows up to watch another player. He ends up signing Roy.

Roy's parents are dead, and he's living with his grandmother, and a big winter storm blows the roof off her farmhouse -- that first check from the Dodgers comes in handy. At Spring Training, Roy continues to be the Good Kid; he hopes to impress the manager enough to be sent to some farm club so he can give his grandmother more money than he'd be getting at the drug store.

There's a veteran catcher at spring training --- Dave Leonard, hoping to hang on so he can make $12,500 for a few seasons until his insurance kicks in. Dave gives Roy a few magic tips, among them:

"Son, an old umpire once give me some dope when I was breaking in like you. Oh, yeah, I thought I was hot stuff, but they soon showed me I didn't have an idea what it was all about. Just when I got convinced I was a flop and waiting for that pink slip in the mailbox, this old fella took me aside in the lobby of the hotel one night. Old George Connors, I never forgot. So I pass it along to you and don't you forget it either. 'Courage,' says this old-timer. 'Courage is all life. Courage is all baseball. And baseball is all life; that's why it gets under your skin.'"

Roy has courage, and soon enough Roy has technique. And Roy becomes a rookie sensation, first in spring training and then in the regular season. But after a game, some players are horsing around in the showers. Someone bumps Roy. He falls, lands on his arm, and suddenly the career of the phenom who has won 16 games is a row is over.

Baseball's a funny game, full of life lessons you can't see when they're coming at you. Dave Leonard gets cut from the team. Then the player-manager gets killed in a car crash, and Dave is brought back to manage the slumping Dodgers. He knows Roy is a natural hitter, so he keeps him on the team and uses him as a pinch hitter. And Roy has great success --- in a single season, he's on his second career.

Then comes the inevitable slump. Roy's ready to quit. Dave gives him a tough-love lecture: "Only the game fish swim upstream." And Roy, reinvigorated, embarks on yet another comeback.

The baseball scenes are as exciting as great newspaper reports of hotly contested games. There are passages that take you inside the game of baseball, and then deeper, into the minds of the men who play it. Does it matter that this book is set in the late 1930s, and Joe DiMaggio is a feared opponent and Roy's grandmother still uses coal in her oven? Not at all --- anyone who loves baseball will be rooting for Roy so fervently that this might as well be non-fiction. (As Tunis puts it in a note at the start of the book, "The author wishes to state that all the characters in this book were drawn from real life.")

It's the blend of utter fantasy --- a rookie who helps lead the Dodgers into a World Series against the Yankees --- and no-nonsense realism that earns this series a permanent place in baseball literature. If you've got a kid who cares about baseball, "The Kid from Tomkinsville" is a gift from God; it will set him (or her) on the path of more great Tunis novels.

And if you are looking for respite from this jaded world of ours --- if you're nostalgic for the crack of the bat and the snap of ball against leather and the look of raked dirt against pristine grass --- these books will revive you like no others I know. ∎

BOOKS

HOME

Emily Evans Eerdmans:
"The World of Madeleine Castaing"

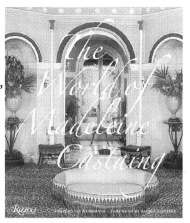

What a beautiful book.

No.

That's too little praise.

What a work of art. What an inspiration.

Look at the American decorating books of the last decade, and what you mostly see is how important it was for the clients --- and their compliant decorators --- to spend tons of money. And they didn't spend it just on the walls and rugs and art and furniture. They went right on to the little things, the chotchkes. Every possible surface has stuff on it; these rooms are busy. Your eye darts around, looking for an idea that centers the space, but there is none. Indeed, none was intended --- the overarching concept here was, apparently, to overwhelm the visitor.

Now let us open "The World of Madeleine Castaing" and consider any of the 275 color and black-and-white illustrations. They're not all the work of Madame Castaing, but the rooms designed by others have her sensibility: simplicity, boldness, originality. The color combinations are like nothing you've ever seen. Often the rooms are almost empty. Instead of a framed painting, you might find that Jean Cocteau has drawn on a wall.

Why isn't Madeleine Castaing a household name?

Because she's impossible to describe in a sound bite.

She was French --- born near Chartres in 1894, dead at age 98 in 1992 --- but you can't really say she was a French decorator. "I can take inspiration from a scene in Chekhov as from a dress by Goya," she said, and she wasn't kidding. In one of her rooms, you could be in Russia, in another room London. Most of the time, the mood she created was timeless, poetic, a fantasy. As she said, "There is always beauty in mystery."

She was, as you might guess, quite a character. Daughter of the engineer who built the Chartres railway station, she was 15 when she saw the 36-year-old man she wanted to marry. She walked right up to him and, in record time, sealed the deal.

In Paris, the Castaings knew everyone, did everything. Most importantly, they started collecting. And not from the approved list. One day they saw students throwing rocks at a gallery window. They moved closer; in the window was a Modigliani nude. They stared for an hour --- and then went in and bought it.

Her husband was tall, handsome and aristocratic. To make sure he didn't stray, she bought a house in Lèves, a lovely village a few miles from Chartres, and set about personalizing it.

World War II took the Castaings by surprise. "We were living in our own world --- we wouldn't even open the letters we got in the mail," she recalled. "All of a sudden soldiers in blue-green got through to the garden and wrecked the bed. My poetic universe had suddenly collapsed."

The Germans occupied the house. The Castaings and their two children moved back to Paris. And as the war ended, Madame Castaing opened her first boutique.

Never had there been a shop like this. For one thing, it did not look like a store --- it was a series of rooms that looked as if someone lived in them. And no two rooms were alike. Indeed, no single room had an identifying theme or style. English Regency tables, Swedish chairs, a Russian couch --- her rooms didn't make statements, they told stories.

The most amusing story about her shop was that Madame Castaing had only modest interest in commerce. As Emily Evans Eerdmans notes, "She opened a shop not because she wanted to sell, but because she liked to buy and make poetic settings out of her acquisitions." So her prices were stratospheric --- she took the real value of her wares and just added a few zeroes. And if she didn't like you, she wouldn't sell to you at any price. On the other hand, a child who told her that a piece was beautiful could have it for almost nothing.

By the 1950s, Madame Castaing was the most admired decorator in Paris. (The gorgeous wallpaper she designed --- there are four dazzling pages of those papers in the book --- is still available, and still looking fresh.) Here too she was a one-off; she gave her clients the rooms she thought they needed, not necessarily the rooms they asked for. By the evidence of this book, there were no complaints.

Until her death, I never made a trip to Paris without visiting 30 rue Jacob, her final location. Her shop was on the first floor; from the street, it looked like an apartment with picture windows. Madame was often on the scene. She was as idiosyncratic as her antiques --- her lips were flaming red, her eyelashes were pasted on, and she wore a wig that announced itself as a fake because she kept it on with a black elastic chin strap. And as she had for decades, she would dress to match her upholstery.

Her family kept the shop going for a decade after her death, and then, in 2004, the contents of her residences and store were auctioned. Life moves on; now there's a branch of Ladurée dispensing pastries at 30 rue Jacob.

You can look at Madeleine Castaing simply as a decorator, and, if you're interested in lovely rooms, you can learn quite a lot from her. Or you can leave the narrowness of occupational identity behind and consider her as an artist and a teacher. What did she have to teach? In essence, this:

Don't be intimidated by audacity. Be audacious --- but with taste... Don't get taken in by fashion. A secret: love your house; love makes miracles.

That's not decorating talk. It's something else. As is this book. ∎

BOOKS

PSYCHOLOGY

Eric Hoffer:
"The True Believer"

"The True Believer" is short: just 168 pages. Eric Hoffer believed in short. Anything that needs to be said, he believed, could be said in 200 words.

Hoffer thought of himself as a writer of sentences, and his book is a collection of remarkable thoughts, simply and precisely expressed. (If you're the kind who reads with a pen in hand, beware --- you could find yourself underlining almost the entire book.)

But what really freaks out any number of readers is that Eric Hoffer (1902-1983) is nobody's ideal of a public intellectual. He barely saw the inside of a school. He spent most of his working life as a longshoreman on the San Francisco docks. Almost every day, he took a three-mile walk. Along the way, thoughts formed. Later they became sentences, then books. Over the years, he wrote ten. "The True Believer" is his masterpiece.

The genius of this book is Hoffer's ability to see beyond individual behavior to patterns of thought and behavior. On page one:

Though there are obvious differences between the fanatical Christian, the fanatical Mohammedan, the fanatical nationalists, the fanatical Communist and the fanatical Nazi, it is yet true that the fanaticism which animates them may be viewed and treated as one... However different the holy causes people die for, they perhaps die basically for the same thing.

Whoa. Let's unpack that.

What Hoffer is saying: All zealots are the spiritual brothers of the Nazi, of bin Laden, of Stalin, of the KKK.

Why does Hoffer make such a blanket condemnation?

All mass movements generate in their adherents a readiness to die and a proclivity for united action; all of them... breed fanaticism, enthusiasm, fervent hope, hatred and intolerance; all of them are capable of releasing a powerful flow of activity in certain departments of life; all of them demand blind faith and single hearted allegiance. All movements, however different in doctrine and aspiration, draw their early adherents from the same types of humanity; they all appeal to the same types of mind.

As an idea, this is a glass of cold water to the face of all those who believe so strongly in a cause that they want everybody else to believe in it. That single-mindedness, that intolerance, is the core question of Hoffer's book: what kind of people become fanatics?

The answer is personal. And psychological. Before they believed, Hoffer writes, they felt small, confused, destined for nothing. With belief, they feel strong, certain. Their fanaticism transforms them; losers become winners. ("Faith in a holy cause is to a considerable extent a substitute for the lost faith in himself.")

Lost people attaching themselves to a passing raft --- if the cause sounds almost randomly chosen, it is. ("In pre-Hitlerian times, it was often a toss up whether a restless youth would join the Communists or the Nazis.")

The goal of the mass movement doesn't matter? Not according to Hoffer. He says: the more unrealistic and unattainable, the better. It's not even important that the doctrine be understood. In fact, Hoffer says, the harder it is to believe, the better. The zealot says: Forget your mind, trust your heart --- and his followers do just that. ("We can be absolutely certain only about things we don't understand.")

You and I know that change is the one immutable law of life, that there are always at least two opinions, that we'll probably die not knowing the ultimate answers. Not so the members of mass movements. They know it all. ("A mass movement...must act as if it had already read the book of the future to the last word. Its doctrine is proclaimed as a key to that book.")

Textbook Hoffer: "A movement can exist without a God but no movement can exist without a devil." And at home and abroad, we have quite a few zealots who also have a genius for identifying "devils" and turning them into "The Other." If you read "The True Believer," you'll understand how they think. ∎

BOOKS

SPIRITUALITY

John O'Donohue

"Endings seem to lie in wait," John O'Donohue wrote. His certainly did. He died in his sleep, January 4, 2008, on vacation near Avignon. He was just 53.

I met John O'Donohue shortly after I read "Anam Cara: A Book of Celtic Wisdom," the 1997 book that made him deservedly famous. "Read" is wrong. At 100 words a minute, I had, over weeks, absorbed enough of this deceptively simple exploration of "soul friendship" to grasp that here was an original thinker, a gifted poet and, most astonishing of all, a philosopher who had forged a way of looking at the world that was painfully aware of human frailty but insistent on the triumphal power of divine love. And he wrote beautifully.

A book this exciting, you have to talk about it. I mentioned O'Donohue to Sarah Ban Breathnach, the author of the Oprah-annointed "Simple Abundance." As luck would have it, she and O'Donohue were friends. And when he came through New York, Sarah generously arranged a dinner.

That was the night I learned to drink single malt.

And was there ever a better teacher in the art of sipping than an Irish philosopher and mystic who had worn the collar for 19 years? I don't recall what we talked about, and neither can my wife, who does not drink; all I remember is the cascades of laughter, the unbuckled happiness of people who are thrilled to be alive, and together, and sharing good fellowship with sympathetic souls in a nice restaurant on a rainy New York night.

An evening like that is so rare I think of it as a religious experience. John O'Donohue, a holy man if ever there was one, had a lot of nights like that. A recent interviewer wrote, in memoriam, about a morning when O'Donohue came to breakfast with a hangover, having polished off an entire bottle of single malt with friends the night before. "The bottle didn't die," he announced, "without spiritual necessity."

That offhand remark was quintessential O'Donohue. He never failed to connect the worldly with the sacred --- and see it all as holy. As a writer and a man, he reminded me of the priest who was a friend of Proust's. Yes, he believed there was a Hell. But he didn't believe anyone went there.

Where do our deepest beliefs come from? Generally from childhood, and then not from what our parents and teachers say, but from what they do and who they are. In John O'Donohue's case, his mother was the family's loving center. His father was a stonemason and farmer --- and, O'Donohue thought, the "holiest man I ever met, priests included." Sometimes the boy would bring tea to his father as he worked the fields. Often, young John heard him --- praying --- before he saw him.

O'Donohue had a superlative education, earned a Ph.D. in philosophical theology from the University of Tubingen, became known as an expert on Hegel and, later, Meister Eckhart. As a priest, he loved the Church's sacramental structure and its mystical and intellectual traditions. He also loved writing. Eventually, an officious bishop made him choose. "The best decision I ever made was to become a priest," O'Donohue would say, years later, "and I think the second best decision was to resign from public priestly ministry."

In fact, he had his issues with Catholicism, especially its views on sex and women. The Church, he said, "is not trustable in the area of Eros at all." And it "has a pathological fear of the feminine --- it would sooner allow priests to marry than it would allow women to become priests."

He was just as hard on other denominations. Religious fundamentalists, he said, "only want to lead you back, driven by nostalgia for a past that never existed, to manipulate and control you... [Their] God tends to be a monolith and an emperor of the blandest singularity." New Age spirituality, he felt, was a smorgasbord, and undisciplined. Not that he found any comfort in secular life. He scorned the mall, feared for the spiritual health of the young, and had a special dislike for media folk, "non-elected custodians of sensationalism."

His bedrocks were his faith and "the Celtic imagination," which, he said, "represents a vision of the divine where no one or nothing is excluded." The blend he created was pure joy: "I think the divine is like a huge smile that breaks somewhere in the sea within you, and gradually comes up again."

O'Donohue was no Pollyanna. He was deeply troubled by bad things happening to good people. But he also saw that "a lot of suffering is just getting rid of dross in yourself, and lingering and hanging in the darkness is often --- I say this against myself --- a failure of imagination, to imagine the door into the light."

So it makes sense that O'Donohue's last book would be nothing but invocations and blessings --- a simple, how-to guide that, in effect, takes him back to his father praying in the fields. By the fact that we live, we are blessed; by the light that shines in our hearts, we have the power to bless others and be blessed by them. Is there a purer, more elementary form of the divine in action?

He asks: What is a blessing? His first answer is formal, and expected: "A blessing is a circle of light drawn around a person to protect, heal and strengthen." But then the poetry enters: "It is a gracious invocation where the human heart pleads with the divine heart." And then there's the magical factor: "When a blessing is invoked, a window opens in eternal time."

We need to impact one another's lives in this spiritual way, he writes, because the process of living in a post-industrial, media-drenched world moves us further and further from our innate wholeness. Only direct action can breach the distance. Happily, it takes no special training to bless one another. It's just a matter of gathering yourself --- and finding the words.

In "To Bless the Space Between Us," the poet in O'Donohue seeks to break the shackles of dead language. He offers fresh blessings, and on topics the Church might overlook --- not just for a new home, marriage and child, but for the parents of a criminal, for parents who have lost a child, for those experiencing exile, solitude and failure.

These blessings look hardship in the face, but only as a challenge. In our souls, and, especially, in our hearts, O'Donohue believed, we are all home. We never left, we never will. How hard it is to hold that thought. And yet, when we take the care of others into our hearts, something happens.....

You may not have a problem with the plainspoken language of O'Donohue's blessings. I do. Maybe it's just a writer's discomfort with another writer's words. But the invocations that dot the book --- my God, can this man write! Just one example:

Our longing for the eternal kindles our imagination to bless. Regardless of how we configure the eternal, the human heart continues to dream of a state of wholeness, that place where everything comes together, where loss will be made good, where blindness will transform into vision, where damage will be made whole, where the clenched question will open in the house of surprise, where the travails of life's journey will enjoy a homecoming. To invoke a blessing is to call some of that wholeness upon a person now.

Death was nothing to John O'Donohue --- a silent friend who walks beside us all our days. And on the other side? "I believe that our friends among the dead really mind us and look out for us," he wrote. "Often there might be a big boulder of misery over your path about to fall on you, but your friends among the dead hold it back until you have passed by."

Let it be. ■

Pema Chodron: "When Things Fall Apart: Heart Advice for Difficult Times"

Deirdre Blomfield-Brown went to Miss Porter's School and graduated from Berkeley. She married, moved to New Mexico, became a teacher, had children. Nothing spectacular occurred to her -- until the day in 1972 when her husband announced that he was having an affair and wanted a divorce.

As so often happens in that moment, her life "fell apart."

"I couldn't feel any ground under my feet," she recalls. "It was devastating."

One day, in a friend's pickup truck, Blomfield-Brown saw a magazine that lay open to an article by Chögyam Trungpa. The title: "Working with Negativity." The first line: "There's nothing wrong with negativity."

Blomfeld-Brown, then 36 years old, took this to mean: "There's nothing wrong with what you're going through. It's very real, and it brings you closer to the truth."

It was, she says, "the first sane advice I had heard for someone in my situation. As I read, I kept nodding and saying to myself: 'This is true.' I didn't even know that Chögyam Trungpa was a Buddhist teacher, or that it was Buddhism I was reading about."

Four years later, Deirdre Blomfield-Brown had taken Chogyam Trungpa Rinpoche as her teacher and was an ordained Buddhist monk: Pema Chodron. In 1984, she would become head of the Gampo Abbey in Nova Scotia. Now this grandmother of three is the best-known American -- man or woman -- writer on Tibetan Buddhism.

But that's too limiting.

Pema Chodron may be a Buddhist scholar, but she doesn't talk or write like one. In "When Things Fall Apart: Heart Advice for Difficult Times," she rarely uses technical terms. She comes across like your smart, no bullshit next-door neighbor. And she pierces all your armor.

We don't get, she says, that fear is our friend. Or that it's "a natural reaction to moving closer to the truth." Instead, "we freak out when there's even the merest hint of fear." Which only makes our situation worse. And then everything falls apart -- "we run out of options for escape."

This is an important moment, she argues. Because this crisis isn't just a test, it's a healing. We can, we think, "solve" the problem. Only we can't. And the sooner we learn that, the sooner we'll feel better. Things don't really get solved. They come together and they fall apart. Then they come together and fall apart again. It's just like that. The healing comes from letting there be room for all of this to happen: room for grief, for relief, for misery, for joy.

She tells a story: A poor family had one son. They loved him beyond measure. He was thrown from a horse and crippled. Two weeks later, the army came to the village and took every able-bodied man to fight in the war. The young man was allowed to stay behind with his family.

The moral: "Life is like that. We call something bad; we call it good. But really we just don't know."

One thing she says we do know: "To stay with a broken heart, with a rumbling stomach, with the feeling of hopelessness and wanting to get revenge -- that is the path of true awakening."

Very Thich Nhat Hanh: Let this moment be your teacher.

Or, in her words: "Spiritual practice is your life, twenty-four hours a day."

Her solution: Abandon hope -- it's a way of denying the present moment. Stop fighting the fact that you will die, stop seeing pain as punishment and pleasure as a reward. Learn to accept obstacles as friends. And accept that "nothing ever goes away until it has taught us what we need to know."

Is there a commercial for Buddhism in these pages? A small one --- she doesn't preach. There is a larger one for meditation. It is not, however, the most urgent commercial. That message? Be kinder to yourself. And then let your kindness flood the world.

Feeling lost and weary, hurt and confused? Pema Chodron would say: What an opportunity to be more alive! Seems crazy. But that's because I'm forced to paraphrase. Give her 148 pages, and you'll see how Pema Chodron makes a great deal of sense. And, more to the point, you'll see how you can open your heart, relax and feel some peace.■

Thich Nhat Hanh

Thich Nhat Hanh doesn't use a telephone, so when I interviewed him, I had to pick him up and drive him to the office. Because he practices "walking meditation," he walks very slowly, breathing very consciously, so every breath and step become prayers.

I knew this. And walked very slowly. But not slowly enough. Every ten paces, I had to stop and go back.

That is not because I am a speedwalker, but because I'm not truly mindful. My loss. For as he points out:

The Buddha confirmed that it is possible to live happily in the here and the now --- even if you still have lots of pain and sorrow within yourself. Mindful breathing helps you become fully alive. And when you are really there, you can touch all the wonders of life that are available in this very moment for your enjoyment...for your nourishment...and for your healing.

This is a very happy man presenting a joyous view of life. You think Buddhism is nihilistic because it lacks a God-figure and does not offer a roadmap to eternal life? Well, listen to this:

This body is not me. I am much more than this body. The space of 50 or 60 or 70 years is not my lifespan. It is not true that I did not exist before I was born. It is not true that I will no longer exist after the disintegration of this body. My ground of being is the reality of no birth, no death. No coming, no going. It is like water is the ground of being of a wave. The wave might be afraid of being or non-being. But if she knows that she is water, she will lose all her fear. Nothing is born...nothing dies. Birth and death cannot really touch us. If you know that, you will be able to enjoy every second of your daily life --- even if you are in terminal illness.

I take great comfort in those words. And in the notion that meditation can be as simple as a conscious in-breath, a conscious out-breath. And that the key to everything is to be wide-awake --- to be "mindful."

Who is Thich Nhat Hanh? He became a monk in Vietnam at 16. He studied Zen (no, Zen is not just a Japanese strain of Buddhism), but in an "engaged" form, so, in the early 1960s, he founded the School of Youth for Social Services --- a Vietnamese Peace Corps --- to help his war-battered countrymen. A university and a magazine followed.

In 1966, his non-violent appeals caused him to be exiled from Vietnam. He taught at Columbia University, then founded a retreat in rural France called Plum Village. Now he comes to America and gives lectures in a voice so quiet and peaceful you have to lean in to hear him.

His themes resonate deeply for me:

Do not be bound to any doctrine, theory, or ideology, even Buddhist ones... Avoid being narrow-minded... Truth is found in life and not merely in conceptual knowledge.... Do not force others to adopt your views... Do not avoid contact with suffering.... Do not maintain anger or hatred... Do not live with a vocation that is harmful to humans and nature.

Dreamer? He's the ultimate realist. "Do not believe that I feel that I follow these precepts perfectly," he says. "I know I fail in many ways. However, I must work toward a goal. These are my goals. No words can replace practice, only practice can make the words."

Yes, but words help. ■

Jaimal Yogis:
"Saltwater Buddha: A Surfer's Quest to Find Zen on the Sea"

Jaimal Yogis hit puberty in Sacramento and freaked out. His peer group was rich, bored kids who got into rich, bored, First World trouble: drugs, vandalism, driving drunk, probation.

Eventually Jaimal decided he'd had enough, and, like the young Siddhartha, left home to see what the real world offered. With a few differences: he "borrowed" $900 from his mother's credit card and flew to Hawaii to become a surfer. Luckily for him — and us — he's sincere and charming. You like him. You want it to work out for him.

Yogis dives into Buddhism. The reading. Sitting. The monastery life, at Thich Nhat Hanh's retreat in France, in India, in California. He lives simply; drugs and alcohol fall away. He gains some wisdom. He becomes artful as a surfer. He gets — bet you didn't see this coming — a master's degree in Journalism from Columbia University.

The joy of "Saltwalter Buddha" is its lightness. There are great surfer stories and great Buddhism stories. There are false starts and unexpected breakthroughs. There is charm and wit to spare. And when it comes to wisdom, Yogis heads right for the big stuff — and nails it. Like this:

On this particular day, the waves were like endless frothy barricades. I'd been paddling for twenty minutes and I still wasn't outside. I pushed and pumped and heaved and whined. The sea punched and kicked and jammed sand down my throat. And in the midst of this abuse, I realized how much I loved surfing.

I loved the actual riding of the wave, of course. But I also loved the challenge of the paddle.

It wasn't always like that. And maybe I was just happy to be back in the water after living in India for months. Or maybe my mind was more accepting after hanging with all the ultra-happy Tibetan monks. But the more I thought about it, the more I realized every surfer has to like paddling, at least a little.

This was because extremely little of each surf session is spent actually standing up on your surfboard on a wave — maybe one percent —- so if you're looking to have a good time it's essential to find a way to enjoy paddling, or at least good naturedly bear it. And in that way, I thought surfing is kind of a good metaphor of the rest of life.

The extremely good stuff — chocolate and great sex and weddings and hilarious jokes — fills about a minute portion of an adult lifespan.

Empirical knowledge. Real knowledge. Very welcome knowledge. ∎

BOOKS

POETRY

SHARON OLDS

Her father is dying, and her plane's
been cancelled, but there's another,
leaving in just a few minutes, not in this
terminal, but it will get her to her father
before he dies, and so Sharon Olds runs
as no woman has ever run before.

Strike Sparks
Selected Poems, 1980–2002

She's making love. Though it looks like she's
having sex, because the writing is so specific.
But as much as Sharon Olds revels in what he does to her, she's not just thinking
about the act but about its meaning. ("How do they do it, the ones who make love
without love?" she wonders.)

Her son, he's so big now. How did it happen? When? And her daughter --- brushing
her hair, Sharon Olds can't help thinking: What does it all mean?

Parents, lovers/husbands, children. Sharon Olds deals mostly --- I could almost say:
deals only --- with the big topics. At least, the big topics if you have parents, hus-
bands/lovers and kids.

The subject of a lot of poetry is poetry: the poem taking its place --- or wanting to ---
in the great chain of literature. Sharon Olds has done her reading. And she has her
influences. But the beauty of her writing is that you see none of that. All you get is a
woman, looking and listening, and then talking. "Do what you are going to do, and
I will tell you about it," she writes at the end of a poem about her parents, and that's
the strength of her work --- it's just the facts she thinks you need, plus her take on
them.

Sharon Olds does not read newspapers or watch TV. "The amount of horror one
used to hear about in one village could be quite extreme," she explains. "But one
might not have heard about all the other villages' horrors at the same time." Also,
she doesn't drink coffee or smoke, and she limits her wine. Her life is marriage,
kids, work. Which, she says, accounts for accessibility of her poems:

*I think that my work is easy to understand because I am not a thinker. How can I put it?
I write the way I perceive, I guess. It's not really simple, I don't think, but it's about ordinary things -- feeling about things, about people. I'm not an intellectual, I'm not an abstract thinker. And I'm interested in ordinary life. So I think that our writing reflects us.*

"Strike Sparks" is a selection of her poems from 1980 to 2002. It tells a story, though that wasn't her intent along the way. ("I'm just interested in human stuff like hate, love, sexual love and sex. I don't see why not.") In these poems, we follow the dying of a father, the growth of children, the deepening of love through sex.

Let me not cast Sharon Olds as the literary equivalent of a thriller writer who can swear like a sailor. Her observations are often small and wry, what you might find in a newspaper column:

> *Whenever I see large breasts*
> *on a small woman, these days, my mouth*
> *drops open, slightly.*

On to "Stag's Leap." When she was 55 and had been married for 32 years, her husband announced that he had fallen in love with another woman and was leaving her. That was devastating for Olds --- she had often written about her marriage, and for those who read her poems as a diary, it was passionate and profound. Now, reflexively, she began to write again. She made one promise, and it was to her two adult children: I won't publish anything for a decade.

Fifteen years later, she published "Stag's Leap. " The reference is to her husband's favorite wine. Equally, that stag jumping off a cliff was a metaphor for her husband's exit: "When anyone escapes, my heart/ leaps up. Even when it's I who am escaped from/ I am half on the side of the leaver." Those lines set a tone. She's not sticking pins in her husband's back and muttering voodoo – she is coming to terms, she is working to see how they have both gone wrong, how she has been a partner in this. Even in "The Last Hour," when you

expect self-control to be lost:

> *Suddenly, the last hour*
> *before he took me to the airport, he stood up,*
> *bumping the table, and took a step*
> *toward me, and like a figure in an early*
> *science fiction movie he leaned*
> *forward and down, and opened an arm,*
> *knocking my breast, and he tried to take some*
> *hold of me, I stood and we stumbled,*
> *and then we stood, around our core, his*
> *hoarse cry of awe, at the center,*
> *at the end, of our life.*

Sharon Olds won the 2012 T.S. Eliot prize for these poems. The vote was unanimous. As Britain's Poet Laureate Carol Ann Duffy, chair of the judging panel, said: "This was the book of her career. There is a grace and chivalry in her grief that marks her out as being a world-class poet. I always say that poetry is the music of being human, and in this book she is really singing. Her journey from grief to healing is so beautifully executed."

Olds is eloquent about what she learned in the writing of these poems:

We'd had a lot of good years; then our lives slowly changed, our characters changed, and we were not so well suited to each other anymore. He just realized it long before me. As I began to be able to see some of what happened (not all) from his point of view—his wish to be with someone more like himself, someone not a writer—then I didn't feel like a victim but more like an equal.

As one of the poems in "Stag's Leap" says: "50/50 we made the marriage/ 50/50 its demise."

Or as she writes in the final lines of the last poem: "I did not leave him, he did not leave me, I freed him, he freed me."

Long ago, Sharon Olds said, "I want a poem to be useful." For anyone in a failing or failed relationship, these poems are nothing less than a lifesaver, a revelation, a cleanser --- a short cut to a clearer future. ■

RUMI

The greatest Muslim poet was born in what is now Afghanistan, back when Muslims, Hindus and Buddhists lived peacefully together.

His funeral lasted 40 days, and he was mourned by Christians, Jews, Muslims, Persians and Greeks.

Okay, Rumi was born in 1207 and died in 1273. That turns out to have been a turbulent era --- but there's not a word about discord in his poems. And there's no record of any criticism coming his way because he was a Sufi and a scholar of the Koran.

Indeed, at his funeral, Christians proclaimed, "He was our Jesus!" while Jews cried, "He was our Moses!"

Both were right. Rumi belongs to everyone. And always will. It makes perfect sense that this 13th century Muslim is now said to be the best-selling poet in 21st century America.

His father was rich, a Sufi mystic and theologian. There's a famous story of Rumi, at 12, traveling with his father. A great poet saw the father walking ahead and Rumi hurrying to keep up. "Here comes a sea followed by an ocean," he said.

Rumi studied, became a noted scholar. Then, when he was 37, he met Shams of Tabriz, a thorny personality. But Shams was God-intoxicated; nothing else mattered. And so their meeting was catalytic. As Rumi said: "What I had thought of before as God I met today in a human being."

He dropped everything to be with Shams. Then Shams disappeared. Later, he reappeared --- only to be murdered, probably by Rumi's jealous son. But by then Rumi was also God-obsessed, and he understood: Between lovers, there can be no separation:

> *Why should I seek?*
> *I am the same as he.*
> *His essence speaks through me.*
> *I have been looking for myself.*

Rumi produced 70,000 verses --- but he never actually wrote a poem. Pressed by a friend to record his thoughts, he pulled out some lines he'd scribbled. "More!" begged Husameddin Celebi. Rumi's response: "Celebi, if you consent to write for me, I will recite." And Rumi began to dictate.

Rumi sometimes called out poems as he danced. As Celebi would write: "He never took a pen in his hand while composing. Wherever he happened to be, whether in the school, at the hot springs, in the baths or in the vineyards, I would write down what he recited. Often I could barely keep up with his pace, sometimes, night and day for several days. At other times he would not compose for months, and once for two years there was nothing. At the completion of each book I would read it back to him, so that he could correct what had been written."

As a poet, Rumi was as clear as he was deep. His story-poems are riddles you can solve. His poems are little telegrams, straight from his heart to yours. Whatever it cost him to write is hidden. His point is: Here is honey. Taste. Eat.

And is there ever nourishment in his work! Consider:

> No matter how fast you run,
> your shadow more than keeps up.
> Sometimes it's in front.
> Only full, overhead sun diminishes your shadow.
> But that shadow has been serving you!
> What hurts you, blesses you.
> Darkness is your candle.
> Your boundaries are your quest.

Don't mistake straightforward speech for simplicity; Rumi is as brain-busting as Zen. For example:

> Why do you stay in prison
> when the door is so wide open?

Which reminds me of a story Rumi tells: A friend sends a prayer rug to a man in prison. What the man wanted, however, was a key or file --- he wanted to break out. Still, he began to sit on the rug and pray. Eventually he noticed an odd pattern in the rug. He meditated on it --- and realized it was a diagram of the lock that held him in his cell. Escape came easily after that...

Escape comes more easily after you read these poems. You may well find yourself, like Rumi, saying:

Where did I come from, and what am I supposed to be doing?
I have no idea.
My soul is from elsewhere, I'm sure of that.
And I intend to end up there. ■

MUSIC

BLUES

Buddy Guy

Eric Clapton called him the "greatest blues guitarist ever." Rod Stewart volunteered to be his valet. Jimi Hendrix said, "Heaven is lying at his feet while listening to him play guitar."

Buddy Guy came to Chicago from Louisiana: "I was so far out in the country, man. We didn't have running water, no electric lights, no radio, and I didn't know nothing about no electric guitar. We used to get the catalogs, like from Sears, and that's how our mother would order our clothes. Didn't have no stores there to buy clothes from."

He started playing professionally in Baton Rouge, won a contest, headed north. In the early 1960s, when some of the best Chicago blues records were made, he was a session guitarist; anything fancy he played was mixed down.

By the mid-1960s, Buddy Guy was Jimi Hendrix before there was a Hendrix; he would pick the guitar with his teeth and play it over his head. (One night Hendrix came, stood in the front row and taped Guy's performance so he could go to school on it.)

At the same time, Buddy Guy was Clapton before there was a Clapton. In fact, the young British bluesman got the idea for Cream as a power trio from Buddy Guy. And as for Cream's music, well.... "You know that Cream tune, 'Strange Brew'?" Guy has recalled. "Eric and I were having a drink one day, and I said, 'Man, that Strange Brew... you just cracked me up with that note.' And he said 'You should... 'cause it's your licks.'"

By the time anyone in Chicago understood or appreciated what Buddy Guy was playing, others had patented that sound. He made a few authentic Chicago records, then languished without a record contract for a decade. By his third or fourth rediscovery, he was old enough to be a grandfather --- and by then, he had moved beyond pure blues to a kind of showmanship that upstaged the music.

But there was a window --- a few years in the mid-1960s --- when Buddy Guy had it all: a powerful set of songs, masterful compatriots, a willing record label. You can hear him in those glory days as the wingman for Junior Wells in that harmonica player's electrifying and flawless "Hoodoo Man Blues." (For contractual reasons, he's billed on early editions of that record as "Friendly Chap.") And then, in 1968, he made a debut record that is nothing less than a primer of Chicago blues.

On "A Man and the Blues," the music has been mixed so Buddy Guy is front and center, and he is never less than dazzling. He plays a single note and lets it hang until it drops out of hearing range. Or he'll rain notes down like bullets, a staccato assault on your ears. But he never plays anything just for show --- everything is in the service of the song. And he's backed by great musicians, especially Fred Below on drums and Otis Spann on piano. Here's a challenge: On slower songs, tune everyone else out and listen to what Spann and Below are playing. It may be blues, but it's as least as subtle as jazz.

There are fast songs that get toes tapping and the heart pumping, especially the Motown hit "Money (That's What I Want)" and "Mary Had a Little Lamb." But it's the slow stuff that takes your breath away. "What can a man do/when the blues keep following him around?" he asks. "So many ways you can get the blues," he moans. He's sitting "a million miles from nowhere" in a shack by the cotton fields. But he's a man. And so he looks for a man's solution: "I'm gonna find me some kind of good woman/Even if she's dumb, deaf, crippled or blind."

It's lonely, lonely stuff --- it's the very definition of the blues. "Give me a little piano now, Spann," he cries, and in comes a glissando as delicate as Chopin and twice as heartbreaking. Makes you want to reach for a cigarette and a whiskey, even if you don't smoke or drink.

Don't feel sorry for Buddy Guy --- over the years, he's sold millions of records, won Grammys, achieved the status of a legend. Now he's the sole survivor of the Chicago greats.

Before he left home, Buddy Guy's father told him, "Son, don't be the best in town. Just be the best until the best come around." But no one I can think of has ever come around with anything better than "A Man and the Blues." ■

ETTA JAMES

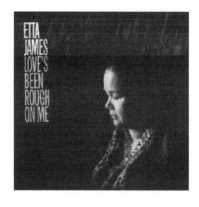

Talk about "born to sing the blues." She was born when her mother was 14 and completely uninterested in the parenting grind.

Her childhood, she said, was like a series of one-night stands; she was passed from relative to relative. The one constant was singing. At five, she joined a gospel choir in Los Angeles --- and was soon proclaimed a prodgy. At 15, she and two friends formed a vocal trio. They got noticed --- their recording of "Roll With Me, Henry" (a title so sexy it had to be renamed: "The Wallflower") went to #2 on the R&B charts. Etta was, at 16, touring with Little Richard.

Her follow-up single, "Good Rockin' Daddy," was another hit. It took her only a few more years to get to Chess Records, the Chicago-based label that knew how to get great records out of blues artists. At 22, Etta James had a big voice --- and a big, brassy personality. And she had History; she'd been a professional musician for six years, she'd been around.

Leonard Chess liked "triangle" songs, and he found a great one for Etta's Chess debut: "All I Could Do Was Cry." The set-up: Etta watching her lover marry another woman. The refrain: "I was losing the man that I loved, and all I could do was cry." Etta needed only one take. When she was finished, she was crying --- and so were some of the engineers.

Success can be harder than failure, especially for musicians.

Etta's response to busted romance was to take drugs. "Some people can't work high, but I can," she boasted. "I may be one of those singers who has enough power to overcome the fog and filters of drugs." She couldn't overcome the cost of drugs, however; she was arrested for writing bad checks.

But she kept pumping out the hits: "I'd Rather Go Blind" and "Tell Mama." After a few lost years, Etta re-connected with Chess Records. By 1978, she was the opening act for the Rolling Stones.

I own most of the Etta James catalogue. I sample it often, for a woman who lived this hard --- who loved and lost and paid the price for everything she got and a lot she didn't --- oozes the kind of wisdom you don't find in books. That was the thing about Etta: She had total credibility. She lived the blues, and you'd best believe she was going to tell you about them, and in the bluntest (and thus, most poetic) way possible. (If you ever saw Etta live, you know that she was a great deal raunchier than the new kids.)

"The blues is my business, and business is good," she sings, and that's true of all the CDs she released since 1989. For me, the best is "Seven Year Itch." After that, it's a coin toss. "Life, Love and the Blues" is pretty great. Of equal merit, "Love's Been Rough on Me."

Jealousy, anger, revenge ("feel like breakin' up somebody's home"), lust --- this is Shakespearean stuff. So lower the lights. Stop all conversation. Etta James was a considerable presence. To hear her is to be shaken, stirred and --- not least --- schooled. ∎

ALBERT KING

One of 13 children. As a child in Arkansas, picked cotton. Grew up to be 6'4", 250 pounds on a thin day. Known to carry a .45 in his waistband.

Think Albert King had an attitude?

You bet. And good for him. Attitude is the first qualification for a Blues musician.

> *Born under a bad sign*
> *Been down since I was old enough to crawl*
> *If it wasn't for bad luck*
> *I wouldn't have no luck at all.*

Lines delivered with total credibility. And not a wasted word.

But for concise elegance we look to his guitar playing. Left-handed. Played a Gibson Flying V with a thumb rather than a pick.

And he used that thumb sparingly.

"It ain't how many notes you play," he said. "It's how you play them."

Guitar players revered him. Mike Bloomfield, no slouch himself: "Albert can take four notes and write a volume. He can say more with fewer notes than anyone I've ever known."

King played in obscurity for much of his career. He worked construction. Saturday nights he was onstage in a dive.

> *I can't read, haven't learned how to write*
> *My whole life has been one big fight*
> *Born under a bad sign*

When he signed with Stax/Volt, everything changed. His new label craved hits, not albums --- the goal was 3-minute songs with hooks. King obliged, and that is how, in 1967, Stax released one of the greatest Blues albums ever, "Born Under A Bad Sign."

Life changed fast. Cream recorded the title song. As did Hendrix. In 1968, rock promoter Bill Graham proposed to pay King $1,600 for three nights at the Filmore in San Francisco. "I hadn't made $1,600 for three days in my life," King would recall.

Graham booked him with Jimi Hendrix and Janis Joplin. The line was around the block; the show moved to a larger theater. The gig was extended --- for three weeks --- and Albert King had a new audience: white kids. A year later, he was performing with the St. Louis Symphony Orchestra, which he described as "an 87-piece blues band."

What he does sounds so simple. *Play less, let every note count.* It's a code we all might consider, though few have the courage to live it --- there's nothing shiny, nothing that grabs people by the lapels, in this approach.

> *Wine and women is all I crave*
> *A big legged woman is*
> *gonna carry me to my grave*
> *Born under a bad sign*

In fact, a heart attack took him. He was 69. Correctly, the Memphis Horns played "When the Saints Go Marching in" at his funeral. ∎

BIG MAMA THORNTON

The first night she sang at Harlem's
Apollo Theater, she was Willie Mae
Thornton, and she was the opening act.
The following night, as "Big Mama"
Thornton, she was the headliner.

That overnight success came in 1952, when Willie Mae was 26. By then, she had
moved far beyond the gospel songs she learned in the churches of Montgomery, Al-
abama, where her father was a minister and her mother sang in the choir. Now she
was living in Houston, performing in clubs, learning to play drums and harmonica,
drinking gin and milk, and being open about her sexuality decades before it was
cool to be a lesbian.

"My singing comes from my experience...my own experience," she said. "I never
had no one teach me nothin'. I never went to school for music or nothin'. I taught
myself to sing and to blow harmonica and even to play drums by watchin' other
people! I can't read music, but I know what I'm singing! I don't sing like nobody
but myself."

Of the 16 songs on the "Ball & Chain" CD, recorded when she was in her early 40s,
two were huge hits --- for others. One was "Hound Dog," which she first recorded
three years before Elvis got to it.

And then there is "Ball N' Chain," which Big Mama wrote and owned until Janis
Joplin started using it as her showstopper.

But the amazing thing about this CD is that these two classics are matched by
almost every other song on it. In part, that's because the musicians playing with her
are world-class. On the first few songs, her band features Buddy Guy (guitar), Walter Horton (harmonica) and the great Fred Below (drums). On two cuts, her only
accompaniment is Fred McDowell's slide guitar. And for six glorious songs, she's
backed by a band that includes Muddy Waters (guitar), James Cotton (harmonica)
and the incomparable Otis Spann (piano).

Mostly, though, what transports you is Big Mama. Her range astonishes. One
moment, she's a crude shouter, loud enough to hush belligerent drunks; the next
moment, she's the repository of all the heartache in the world. You'll listen carefully
to "Sweet Little Angel" because no one's done it better. And you'll want to get up
and dance to "Wade in the Water," because she's singing flat-out gospel against a
pounding tambourine and a scorching guitar. But on the twentieth hearing, or

thereabouts, you will listen to Otis Spann's hushed piano against her forlorn voice in "Life Goes On" and feel something like awe.

Big Mama never knew real success. She got royalties of $500 for "Hound Dog," her first and only commercial hit. She lived hard. She drank more than was good for her. She died in 1984, aged 62, in a Los Angeles rooming house.

Naturally, she's much more popular now than she was when she was alive. ■

HOODOO MAN BLUES
JUNIOR WELLS'
CHICAGO BLUES BAND
with BUDDY GUY

JUNIOR WELLS

He was making $1.50 a week on a soda truck in West Memphis to earn the money for a harmonica. But it cost $2. The pawnshop owner walked away from the counter for a moment, so he stole it. Got arrested. Appeared before the judge.

"Why did you do it?"

"I had to have that harp."

"Yes? Can you play it?"

He took the harmonica and let loose.

"Here's the 50 cents you need," the judge said. "Case dismissed."

Amos Wells, Jr., aged 12, was on his way.

By 14, he was in Chicago, sitting in with blues legends and earning the nickname "Junior." Even as a teen, he had a distinctive style --- when you least expected it, his harmonica produced a blast, just as his singing was punctuated by the occasional yelp. And he instinctively knew that the blues was best as raunchy, sexy music, and that it held dark secrets about the midnight politics between men and women.

He looked the part of a bluesman. Sharkskin suit, slicked hair, sharp hat, cigarette. One night, at a club, he handed a friend a wad of cash to hold while he played --- he couldn't abide an unsightly bulge in his clothes. Another night, a friend and his wife were threatened by some drunk jerk. Junior jumped off the stage and pointed a pistol at the jerk, as his friends wondered, "Where did he hide that gun in his skintight suit?"

He was a character. In some clubs, when his band started to play, Junior was at the bar, which had been rigged with a remote mike so he could perform without having to leave his drink. On the bandstand, his tools awaited: harps in seven keys. And, always, a bottle of gin.

"Hoodoo Man Blues," his first record, and his best, was made in 1965. Buddy Guy plays guitar. Jack Myers plays bass, Billy Warren is on drums. Giants, all. If they sound as if they're in a club, that's deliberate; this is pure Chicago blues, raw as the liquor served in those joints and, in the slower numbers, smooth as the lines of sharp-dressed men working to seduce foxy women. Listen to an overdone song like "Good Morning Little Schoolgirl" --- it's so down and dirty you want to check the lock on your daughter's window.

When Junior died, at 63, he was laid out in a royal blue suit and wide-brimmed hat. In his coffin: harmonicas in every key and a pint of Tanqueray. ∎

MUSIC

CLASSICAL

GREGORIO ALLEGRI: MISERERE

Rome. Easter Week. The year: 1639 or 1790, it's all the same. The Matins service at the Vatican. 3 AM. Twenty-seven candles are lit. One at a time, they're extinguished. One candle left. The Pope kneels before the altar and starts to pray.

Music begins.

And what music! The words are familiar: Psalm 51, David's account of his affair with Bathsheba and his plea to God --- "Wash away all my guilt; from my sin cleanse me." It's the choral work that stuns. Sweeping harmonies for the choir. A top C sung by a single castrato. And, connecting them, the simplest of chants.

This "Miserere" was the glory of Gregorio Allegri (1582 - 1652), known mostly as a singer in the Papal Chapel. For this one work, written in 1638, he joins the immortals --- it is clearly an exquisite piece. It's so excellent, in fact, that one of the 17th century Popes decided it should be played only on Wednesday and Good Friday of Holy Week, and only in the Sistine Chapel. No one dared to copy it; the penalty was excommunication.

Thus begins a remarkable story about Allegri's "Miserere." In 1770, when he was just 14 years old, Mozart and his father came to Rome for Holy Week. St. Peter's and the Sistine Chapel were obvious destinations; on Wednesday, Mozart heard the "Miserere." That night, from memory, he transcribed it.

On Good Friday, he brought his copy --- hidden in his hat ---to the second performance of the piece. When he checked it for accuracy, he discovered he'd made just two mistakes. No copy of the Mozart transcription exists. It's said he handed it off, whereupon it was copied again --- and his version was then destroyed.

The truth of this story? Unknown. But only the music matters. I have heard it, on Good Friday, in a cathedral with wonderful acoustics, and it was ambrosia --- music of such purity that, like David, I felt like a sinner before God. Add incense and priests and squint a little, and you're in Rome, 300 years ago.

In the way great beauty is unsettling, the Miserere is wonderfully disorienting. ■

BACH:
SUITES FOR UNACCOMPANIED CELLO

Considering that the Bach Cello Suites live in the marrow of millions of music lovers, it seems hard to believe that these six masterpieces, written around 1720, went almost completely unperformed until almost 1900. They weren't "lost." They were just regarded as études --- as exercises.

In 1890, 13-year-old Pablo Casals was browsing through scores in an old music shop near the harbor in Barcelona. But let him tell it:

Suddenly I came upon a sheaf of pages, crumbled and discolored with age. They were unaccompanied suites by Johann Sebastian Bach --- for the cello only! I looked at them with wonder: Six Suites for Violoncello Solo. What magic and mystery, I thought, were hidden in those words? I had never heard of the existence of the suites; nobody --- not even my teachers --- had ever mentioned them to me. I forgot our reason for being at the shop. All I could do was stare at the pages and caress them. That sensation has never grown dim. Even today, when I look at the cover of that music, I am back again in the old musty shop with its faint smell of the sea.

I hurried home, clutching the suites as if they were the crown jewels, and once in my room I pored over them. I read and reread them. I was thirteen at the time, but for the following eighty years the wonder of my discovery has continued to grow on me. Those suites opened up a whole new world. I began playing them with indescribable excitement. They became my most cherished music. I studied and worked at them every day for the next twelve years.

Yes, twelve years would elapse and I would be twenty-five before I had the courage to play one of the suites in public at a concert. Up until then, no violinist or cellist had ever played one of the Bach suites in its entirety. They would play just a single section --- a Saraband, a Gavotte or a Minuet. But I played them as a whole; from the prelude through the five dance movements, with all the repeats that give the wonderful entity and pacing and structure of every movement, the full architecture and artistry.

They had been considered academic works, mechanical, without warmth. Imagine that! How could anyone think of them as being cold, when a whole radiance of space and poetry pours forth from them! They are the very essence of Bach, and Bach is the essence of music.

I've read a lot of commentary on the Cello Suites, and I have returned to report that academic questions are of scant interest to me. I doubt you'd care much either. The whole and entire point of the Bach Cello Suites, for modern listeners, is the emotion we hear in this music. With Casals, we find a Bach who "has every feeling: lovely, tragic, dramatic, poetic." He knows how to enter our souls.

Casals made the Suites into meditations. Forget the jaunty beginning and the nod to dance music; to hear Casals is to watch Bach think. What you get is a complete experience --- holistic music, healing music.

What this suggests is that, for the cellist, the Cello Suites are about far more than music. They're a challenge to the cellist's deepest conclusions about life. Mstislav Rostropovich put it bluntly:

The hardest thing in interpreting Bach is the necessary equilibrium between human feelings, the heart that undoubtedly Bach possessed, and the severe and profound aspect of interpretation... You cannot automatically disengage your heart from the music. This was the greatest problem I had to resolve in my interpretation...

The Casals recording is the first; it's not radical to argue that it's the greatest. There are many other interpretations. There's no wrong answer. There is a right one: Life is infinitely poorer without the Cello Suites.■

BEETHOVEN:
VIOLIN CONCERTO IN D

Franz Clement may not have been as great a violinist as Ludwig van Beethoven was a composer, but he was quite the celebrity in 19th century Vienna. As a former prodigy on the violin, he was known for his dazzling showmanship and his ability to memorize great chunks of music without apparent effort.

In the late fall of 1806, the 26-year-old Clement decided to sponsor a benefit concert. The beneficiary: Franz Clement. The program: Handel and Mozart. But Clement needed something more --- an attention-getting premiere. So he asked his 36-year-old friend, Ludwig van Beethoven, to write a violin concerto.

There wasn't much time --- the concert was scheduled for December 23rd --- but Beethoven rose to the challenge. Working with uncommon speed, he is said to have finished his concerto on the day of the performance. Some say that Clement had to sight-read the last movement that night --- and that the ink on his score was still damp.

Beethoven's premiere took second place to Clement's showmanship. The violinist divided the piece, playing part before intermission, part after. And he performed a fantasia that night with his violin upside-down. Beethoven's concerto was easy to overlook --- critics called it common and repetitious.

Between 1806 and 1844, how often was Beethoven's Violin Concerto played?

Three times.

Beethoven died on March 26th, 1827. Between 10,000 and 30,000 people attended his funeral. Few were aware that Vienna's beloved composer had ever written a concerto for violin.

Almost a decade after Beethoven's death, Felix Mendelssohn brought the piece to the public's attention. He understood what Beethoven had written: the only major work for violin composed since Mozart's 1775 burst of five concertos. This time people heard it for what it was --- probably the greatest violin concerto ever written.

Why the greatness? Simple. This is gorgeous, melodic music, from start to finish. The dark, brooding Beethoven? Not present here. This Beethoven is peaceful. He chooses only the most satisfying harmonies. His colors are bright. And he gives the soloist ample opportunity to shine --- and, in the Rondo, the final movement, opportunity to thrill. No hype: For me, this is the most pleasurable 45 minutes in classical music.

What version to recommend? I grew up on David Oistrakh, but that brilliant recording is no longer available. I appreciate Isaac Stern's interpretation, but understand that it's controversial. Anne-Sophie Mutter made her CD when she was just 16; I don't care how precocious she was, I prefer someone who's had a bit more life experience.

Which leads me, inevitably, to Jascha Heifetz (1900-1987), generally known as "the violinist of the century." No recording of the Beethoven concerto will ever be "definitive," but his, made in 1955 with Charles Munch and the Boston Symphony Orchestra, comes close. Also on this CD: Heifitz's recording of the Mendelssohn --- from 1959, again with Munch and Boston. Heifetz, you should know, was regarded as his generation's greatest interpreter of Mendelssohn; there are those who think his version of Mendelssohn's concerto is superior to his Beethoven.

Never has joy come cheaper. ∎

Glenn Gould:
The Goldberg Variations

In 1741, a Russian count who lived in Leipzig had trouble sleeping. To calm his nerves, Count Kaiserling ordered Johann Gottlieb Goldberg, his personal pianist, to play in the next room. And the Count asked Johann Sebastian Bach to provide Goldberg with some clavier pieces --- music that would be soothing but cheerful.

Bach, at the height of his genius, was not about to knock off some insignificant ditties. Instead, he produced what's been described as "the most serious and ambitious composition ever written for harpsichord."

In form, the piece consists of an aria, thirty variations, and a repeat of the aria. The great achievement: Instead of writing variations on the melody, Bach built the piece by embellishing the ground bass line.

The Count loved Bach's music. "Dear Goldberg," he would say, "Do play me one of my variations."

Or so the story goes.

The Count claimed ownership --- he had, after all, paid Bach with a golden goblet filled with a hundred gold pieces --- but this work has never been known as the Kaiserling Variations. For more than two hundred years, it was the Goldberg Variations. And then, in 1955, the cognoscenti dubbed it the "Gouldberg" Variations.

Glenn Could was a certified prodigy. He could read music when he was just 3 years old and was composing at 5; now, at 22, he was about to make his debut for Columbia Records. His choice of music: The Goldberg Variations. And he'd play them not as written, but on a piano.

Gould's recording sessions were instant legend. He had astonishing requirements: the right room temperature, the right chair. Before recording, he would soak his hands and arm to the elbows in hot water for twenty minutes. Eccentric? He hummed as he played. He rocked in his chair until it squeaked. But his interpretation was revolutionary: up-tempo, dramatic, technically dazzling.

No pianist has ever been hyped like Gould. Record of the year? Try the decade. But even that was too small. No sooner had Gould's Goldberg Variations been released than critics were calling it one of the century's greatest recordings. And the world agreed: Gould's recording sold and sold and sold.

Gould's astonishing debut --- imagine if Bruce Springsteen had made "Born to Run" at, say, 15 --- cemented his legend as musician and eccentric. And then he topped himself. In 1981, the now 50-year-old pianist decided to re-record the Goldberg Variations in the same New York studio that was the setting for his 1955 debut.

Pressed for an explanation, Gould cited the advances in technology: stereo, Dolby. But more to the point, he said, he had listened again to his 1955 recording --- and he'd found it "very nice, but 30 interesting, independent-minded pieces going their own way." His self-assessment was harsh: His original recording contained "things that pass for expressive fervor in your average conservatory, I guess."

Some critics find Gould's second recording superior: thoughtful, energetic, the interpretation of a mature artist. Others cite technical glitches and phrasing that couldn't be explained as "eccentric". Clearly, there's no end to debate when the subject is Glenn Gould. But the overarching fact about this 1981 recording overwhelms the critical conversation --- this was Gould's last record. He died just a few weeks after it was released.■

Arvo Part

If you recall how Michael Moore handled the attack on the World Trade Center in "Fahrenheit 9/11," you know that --- to the surprise of those who hate him --- he did it very, very artfully.

Almost a minute of blank screen, with only sound to tell you what's happening. Sounds of the planes hitting the Towers --- sounds you've never heard before --- and the human counterpoint: people screaming. Then we see papers blowing in a smoke-filled sky, an abstract image of loss. And music: Arvo Part's "Cantus In Memory Of Benjamin Britten," a solemn meditation, with bells and solitary voices and silences between notes.

Whoever picked Arvo Part knew what he/she was doing. Because this is holy music --- music that speaks without intermediaries to the soul. It both acknowledges grief and suggests completion. It is, as Part has described it, "like light going through a prism." Which is why, when AIDS first swept across New York City in the 1980s, "Cantus In Memory Of Benjamin Britten" --- from the "Tabula Rasa"' CD --- is said to have been a great favorite of dying men in the final weeks of their lives.

Who is Arvo Part?

First, a child of Estonia, a tiny country across the Baltic Sea from Finland. It became a satellite of the Soviet Union when Part was young. Eventually he left, settling in West Berlin, where he has lived for decades. He's now in his 70s, with a vast number of compositions and recordings.

But place is not important in accessing Arvo Part --- the key fact about him is that he has no real connection to this century. The music tells the story: It is timeless. If you must think of an antecedent, try Bach, for Part and Bach both use religious texts, in Latin. And Part, like Bach, favors a structure that, for all its intricacies, is fundamentally simple --- a prayer to God.

In Part's case, the music is built on what he describes as "tintinnabulation" --- a bell-like repetition of a single note. The music doesn't move forward. It sits. It just... exists. Indeed, if you listen carefully, it becomes the only thing that exists. As Part says:

The complex and many-faceted only confuses me, and I must search for unity. What is it, this one thing, and how do I find my way to it? Traces of this perfect thing appear in many guises --- and everything that is unimportant falls away. Tintinnabulation is like this. Here I am alone with silence. I have discovered that it is enough when a single note is beautifully played. This one note, or a silent beat, or a moment of silence, comforts me.

This is evocative, cinematic music; it's not surprising that, from 1958 to 1967, Part composed music for Estonian film and television. Like the best film scores, his music takes you deeper into the image, makes you look harder and see more. It's expansive, inspiring; as a conductor has noted, it takes a single moment and spreads it out.

Of the many recordings of Part's work available, I prefer the "Te Deum." It is majestic, heartfelt, mysterious, profound, moving. But it's very personal music --- it presses emotional buttons --- and so it may feel very different to you. The good news: You will definitely feel something. There is just no way that music of this depth will fail to reach you --- the only question is how far inside it will take you. ∎

MUSIC

COUNTRY

STEVE EARLE

People who have never heard Steve Earle's music know him as the guy who wrote a song about that kid from California who joined the Taliban. But Earle's hardly "anti-American" --- on the short list of true patriots, he's near the top.

Why did Earle write that song?

"I have a son almost exactly the same age as John Walker Lindh," he told an interviewer. "And for some reason, the way I related to it when I first saw him, you know, duct-taped naked to a board on CNN, I saw an underfed, you know, 21-year-old kid, and I got a kid that looks underfed even when I feed him, and I related to it as a parent. The first thing I thought is, 'He's got parents somewhere.'"

That's not an apology for the kid's views; it's a look inside his head to try and figure out how he came to have those views. Which is how Steve Earle works --- he's always the guy with an oblique slant, a fresh angle. That was a good thing when he hit Nashville in the mid-1980s; the country music machine had run out of stars and was willing to consider someone who didn't color between the lines. So, for a while, Steve Earle was the next Hank Williams, the next Johnny Cash, the next Springsteen.

Nice comparisons, but untrue. He was condemned to be himself: a "hard-core troubadour" with a penchant for politics and a weakness for drugs. So there were six marriages ("You can't say I have a problem with commitment"), jail time for drugs, and, since his release, six CDs in as many years, a book of short stories, a play and innumerable concerts and benefits.

Category: Call him the King of "alt country." But that makes him sound as if he's still wearing a chip on his shoulder--- and the simple fact is, Steve Earle's love songs alone put him in the pantheon. "I still write more songs about girls than I do anything else," he says, and those songs run the gamut from macho-comic ("I Don't Want to Lose You Yet") to the unabashedly heartbreaking ("I Can't Remember If We Said Goodbye").

But yes, of course, there are also political songs. "I was probably 14 when I started going out and playing in coffeehouses in San Antonio," he explains. "That is a very conservative military community, and, therefore, during the Vietnam War, it was extremely polarized, especially as the war wore on and body bags started to come back. It just never occurred to me to separate issues and music."

In the hope that you will fall under his spell, my choice of a starter CD is, perhaps, a curious one: not his most recent release, but his first one. "Guitar Town" is the kickoff of his career, and it begins with lyrics that both acknowledge that and celebrate it: "Hey, pretty baby, are you ready for me/I'm a hard rockin' daddy down from Tennessee." A few lines in, he confesses he's got "a two-pack habit and a motel tan." And just to make sure he's slapped you awake, he offers up the totally incorrect observation: "Everybody said, 'You won't get far/on thirty-seven dollars and a Jap guitar.'" And that's all in just the first song!

The rest of the CD touches all the emotional bases, from parental love to "my old friend the blues." Politics? "I was born in the land of plenty/now there ain't enough," he sings, but not so it would grate. And, on the remastered edition, there's a bonus track: Springsteen's "State Trooper."

If ever there was a "modern classic," this is it. ∎

EMMYLOU HARRIS

Emmylou Harris has many admirers, but my wife and I may be the only ones who chose our wedding date based on her tour schedule.

It wasn't about her --- we wanted Buddy Miller, her lead guitarist, and his wife Julie to give a mini-concert for the guests at our wedding.

We spent just enough time with the Millers that weekend to grill them about Emmylou. They had no dish --- really, they had almost nothing to say about her. And they explained why: Emmylou Harris is an unspeakably nice person.

Her twitches are minor: baseball, her dogs, and if there's a third one, I've forgotten it. After three marriages, she lives in Nashville with her mother and brother. She has a shelter for rescued dogs in her yard.

Her career reads equally saintly. Over 40 years and 25 records and a dozen Grammys, she's followed her instincts, and, in the process, avoided sudden spikes and tumbles. She has graced hundreds of records as a celestial back-up singer and duet partner. The verdict is generous: There are, a critic has said, no bad Emmylou Harris records --- only good ones and better ones.

"Hard Bargain" is one of the better ones. Recorded in just a month with only three musicians, its first distinction is that Emmylou wrote 11 of the 13 songs. This is unusual --- it's only the third release on which she's been the dominant writer. The second distinction is that she's in her 60s now, and, like a lot of people who have attained three score, she can't quite grasp where the time went. And why people who have been important to her --- Gram Parsons and Kate McGarrigle, most prominently --- can be located only in memory.

This is a CD of deep feeling: sad memory, deep loss, specific regret. But it's not self-indulgent or maudlin --- if anything, the music is unusually jaunty. She's reached a place where she can see far and she can see wide without trading sharp observation or wry insight for boomer platitude.

It's tricky to interview an icon. Fame at that level is a shield; you can't get in, she can't get out. It's tough enough with actors. It's much tougher with an Emmylou Harris, because everything about her --- that crystalline voice, that forever gray hair

--- suggests that she's some kind of living saint. When we chatted on the phone, that seemed like a good place to start.

JK: I've been listening to you --- and reading about you --- for decades, and it occurred to me: I know nothing about you that you don't want me to know. How have you achieved that? A flawless life? Or total discretion?

EH: A flawless life, *absolutely*. The only time I ever appeared in the Enquirer was for a piece about people who let their hair grow gray. I guess I'm not much of a wild child.

JK: Buddy Miller says that he feels what he plays is "country" and that stuff they play on the radio is "alternative." Given that he was your guitarist, on and off, for a decade, it's no stretch to say that applies equally to you. Where are you with country music and/or Nashville?

EH: I'm nowhere with country music. I don't hear much of it, so I shouldn't venture an opinion, but when it finds me, it seems formulaic. I don't hear anyone who moves me like George Jones or Bill Monroe. The country that you hear on the radio, it feels poppy but without the originality of pop.

JK: Do you miss your country years?

EH: I had my run. It served me well. Country taught me how to sing, it put me on a path. But I was never going to be locked into a formula. I don't want to be considered a current country artist.

JK: Still, you live in Nashville. Go out much?

EH: I'm going out tonight to present an award to Kris Kristofferson and see a free movie.

JK: What about tomorrow night?

EH: Normally I don't go out. I run a dog rescue shelter.

JK: Topic change: your new CD. On which you do your own backup vocals. Is this a first?

EH: No, but I've never sung backup on all the songs before.

JK: Musically, is it more of a challenge?

EH: As an experience, it's easier to harmonize with yourself than with others. But I still judge it by the same standards --- if I didn't sound good or we needed a different color, we'd bring someone in.

JK: You've spoken of going from gig to gig on your bus: "I'm like a trench soldier, I've been out there on the bus." After all these years, do you ever look at rock stars and think, "I'd kill for their plane?"

EH: I love the bus! You can spread out. You have your books. You can sleep when you want, have company when you feel like it. And you can take your dogs. I wish I'd realized that earlier --- it's only in the last 15 years that I've taken them with me on the bus. They're such a joy --- they keep you in the present.

JK: When I think of you, I think of Virgil's line: "Admire a large vineyard, cultivate a small one." By which I mean: You've always been hungry for the music --- not the fame.

EH: You must have *somebody* listening. I have just enough people paying attention that I have the freedom to be in charge. And I have a great record company --- Nonesuch understands what I'm about.

JK: Paul Simon says, "When I'm in the music, I'm no age." And as a performer, you too have achieved around 40 years of visible past. No surprise that your new CD is drenched in time --- time as a force, almost a character. How heavy does that feel?

EH: Paul's right --- time is light when I'm making music. Other times it ranges from heavy to inconsequential. But the press of time? It's always there. And it's sometimes a wonder --- I can't believe that I'm at this age and still working and have all these things I want to do. In that, I'm lucky. I'm healthy and in better shape than I was 30 years ago.

JK: Energy, creative spark, opportunity --- so why name the CD "Hard Bargain?"

EH: Just being in the world is a hard bargain. Everything has a price, a blessing and a curse. It's relentless. We can't really resist life --- we're pulled back into it.

JK: What's the reward?

EH: The reward is that we're here. ∎

MUSIC
JAZZ

MULATU ASTATKE

The ingredients sound... odd. Mulatu Astatke grew up in Ethiopia but went abroad to study jazz in America. What he brought back to Ethiopia was a blend of soul and jazz. Which he then proceeded to blend, once more, with traditional Ethiopian music.

The result is easy to listen to and hard to describe. The horns play cool jazz figures; you could almost mistake them for clarinets. But under that is a groove that could have been created by Booker T and the MGs. And connecting the two are some Ethiopian chords that sound exotic, space-changing, hypnotic.

Think Ethiopian cha cha. Cuba goes to Memphis. Desert trance music. Like nothing you have ever heard before.

Mulatu Astatke is in charge of all of it: He writes the music, arranges it, and plays piano, organ, vibes and percussion. Although the Golden Years of this Ethiopian music were ancient history --- from 1968 to 1974 --- Astatke is still a major figure in Ethiopian music, regularly playing and teaching.

Happily, Jim Jarmusch is one of those directors who not only listens to a lot of music, but looks for a way to integrate it into his films. "Music often leads me," he says. "I discovered Mulatu Astatke's music maybe seven years ago, and I was blown away by a few things I found that he had recorded in the late sixties. I was on a hunt for a number of years: I bought some vinyl; some of his jazz stuff; some Latin jazz recorded in the states; other Ethiopian stuff. And then I was like, "Oh, man, how can I get this music in a film? It's so beautiful and score-like." Then when I was writing 'Broken Flowers,' I was like, "Well, this neighbor [Jeffrey Wright] is Ethiopian-American, I can turn him on to the music."

There are other musicians on that movie soundtrack --- and four songs by Astatke that are crucial to the feeling of the film. They're certainly crucial to my jaded ears, which perk up as soon as his songs start. And which led me to order more of his music.

You'll want to be the first on your block to hear this music. Not because of the "hip" factor, though I won't pretend that's unimportant. But because of the pure pleasure --- this is very happy music, and happy in a smart way. Each time you listen, you hear a little more. With a hundred encounters, you may actually get what this genius is doing. ∎

John Coltrane

On December 9, 1964, tenor saxophonist John Coltrane and his band recorded
an album that has come to be regarded
as one of the greatest achievements in
jazz.

No, make that: 20th century American music.

Or go further, as many do, and say "A Love Supreme" belongs in the rarest zone
of art, that place where personal history and technical skill and spiritual mastery
merge --- and magic happens. Genius lives there. And saints. And Coltrane's ambition in the last few years of his too-short life was, as he said, "to become a saint."

Count "A Love Supreme" as one of his qualifying miracles.

The music is not jazz as it was played at that time --- even as Coltrane and his group
were playing jazz at that time. It's music that came out of Coltrane's years of drug
addiction, his recovery, his gratitude to God. Over the past four decades, the music
has stunned listeners of every persuasion; many have come to feel that it's less music directed to God than music that's coming from God to his faithful messengers
--- Coltrane, McCoy Tyner (piano), Jimmy Garrison (bass) and Elvin Jones (drums).

"'A Love Supreme' was a testament -- John's testament to a higher power," Tyner
would say later. "His spiritual inclinations were very strong, which means he
believed in something that is more powerful than any of us but is still in all of us.
When we made that recording, it was as if we were saying, 'We're here now, we're
going to play, we're going to praise You.'"

That praise took one evening. It came in the form of a four-part suite that Coltrane
sketchily discussed with his band members that night. They didn't need much conversation --- they'd been playing together for years, they were as intelligent as they
were talented, they listened and cared. No players were better able to keep up with
Coltrane as he traced a spiritual quest through the music --- starting with a mystical
mantra, moving into a ferocious and passionate cry, and coming to completion with
music unheard-of and unimagined by most musicians and players, music that took
the saxophonist to a place so special he and the group would play "A Love Supreme"
in public only once.

The ambition is dazzling. Mozart needed an orchestra and a choir for his "Requiem." Coltrane's effort is four guys and a single voice --- at one point, Coltrane chants, the only time he ever did that on a recording.

You don't have to be a jazz lover to appreciate this. Nor do you have to be a Seeker. You just have to be open and attentive and willing to give 32 minutes to all the musical variations on that four-syllable title. And you have to accept that one of our greatest artists will take his gorgeous, warm tone way beyond "My Favorite Things" --- and get you home safe and at peace.

Small fact: McCoy Tyner, Elvin Jones and Jimmy Garrison each received $142 for this recording. Coltrane got $244, plus royalties. A love supreme, indeed. ■

KEITH JARRETT

Those who love "The Koln Concert" border on fanaticism. They say it redefines jazz, and jazz piano in particular.

And more: those who love it say it both makes us tap our feet and takes us someplace holy. That it teaches us yet again how the spaces between notes aren't just silences, but music. That it is, finally, that rarest of events --- sustained beauty, captured in the moment.

Those who like it less say it's a brilliant trick masquerading as jazz. That Jarrett is a great showman --- sincere in his music, but deluded about its quality. That this is the kind of music very smart college boys use to impress (and seduce) their dates. That, like mediocre Chinese food, it's better when you're high --- and soon leaves you hungry. That it spawned George Winston and hundreds of artistically empty "New Age" CDs.

Why such a schism? Because "The Koln Concert" is, for 66 legendary minutes, completely improvised. Jarrett takes a simple figure and explores it, then starts again, a strategy that requires enormous courage and thinking at super-computer speed if the pianist hopes to avoid cliche --- and Jarrett, astonishingly, does avoid every cliche. For another, it involves so much more than piano. Jarrett is really playing duets with himself; he hums, taps his foot and sighs, and the microphone gets it all.

For me, "The Koln Concert" is a great relief from the music of its period. Jarrett recorded it when "fusion" was all the rage. That loud, aggressive jazz-rock has its fans, but I am not among them. In contrast, I find "The Koln Concert" refreshingly quiet and lyrical. And subtle. It touches all the tender places, but it keeps veering toward optimism and radiance. For that reason alone, it works as dinner music and 9 PM "deep thought" music and late-at-night, go-to-bed music.

Who is Keith Jarrett? A prodigy. Before he was 3, his parents saw he had perfect pitch; at 3, he started taking piano lessons. At 6, an IQ test confirmed he was off the charts; he began school in the third grade. As a teenager, he was playing professionally. Soon enough, he was in Charles Lloyd's band. And then came Miles Davis.

In the early 1970s, Jarrett started playing concerts of solo improvisations. There's no greater high-wire act for a musician; Jarrett's done it for thousand of concerts and dozens of CDs without ever losing his edge. The key factor is, perhaps, less about genius and more about attentiveness.

The irony here is that Jarrett wasn't attentive in Koln --- not, anyway, in his terms. He didn't sleep for two nights before the concert. The piano was a Bosendorfer, not his favorite. He'd had a bad Italian meal. He was, he felt, so unprepared to play that he almost sent the engineers home.

And all of that contributed mightily to the great performance he gave that night in 1975.

I say this because I find Jarrett's music to be about process, about this note and this note and this note. Jarrett doesn't pay rapt attention, he is rapt attention; he's so into the music that he merges with it. If there's a greater argument for mindfulness --- being in the moment --- I don't know it.

That kind of consciousness also tunes the listener's consciousness. An artist takes a technique --- improvisation, in this case --- far beyond its old borders. Inevitably, this pulls his audience to a new place.

Generally, this experience is accompanied by a lot of moaning and an ever-shrinking audience. Not in Keith Jarrett's case. "The Koln Concert" was a huge seller when it was released. It has sold hundreds of thousands of CDs over three decades. It's now a certified classic. It deserves to be --- this is very accessible music. You don't have to know anything about jazz to love it. ∎

Herbie Mann

Herbie Mann was born Herbert Jay Solomon in 1930. He got his first saxophone when he was 9. By 14, he was in a band that played resorts in the Catskills.

In 1953, a stroke of luck: A friend told him a jazz band needed a flute player. Mann had never played a flute; at the audition, he played sax. His flute, he said, was being repaired. Only when he got the job did he take a crash course in jazz flute.

By the late '50s, Mann had his own band and was getting somewhere. Again, good fortune: A friend suggested that he add a conga player. His music changed; he was, suddenly, among the first to draw on international sounds and play what is now known as World Music. And then, in 1962, his band rocked the downtown clubs.

The first song on "At the Village Gate" is "Comin' Home Baby." How often does an almost nine-minute jazz tune reach the top 30 singles? But it was an instant hit on the pop charts. And then the album was a hit, and then it was elevated to the ranks of classic.

Six decades later, here's how cool "Village Gate" is: It could have been made yesterday. That is, if there were a group around that dared to launch "Comin' Home Baby" with a solid minute of stand-up bass playing a single note against subtle bop drums --- a combination that practically forces listeners to get up and strut.

The flute is not usually a jazz instrument. It is here. There's the lilt and trill of songbirds. But even more, there's a killer melody, and Mann drives it hard, turning your walk into an outrageous thrust of hips. "Comin Home Baby" is sexy and smart. "Summertime" and "It Ain't Necessarily So" show how you can take Gershwin into a delightful, Brazilian-tinged zone.

Three songs, one of them indelible, two merely great. Half a million copies sold in the first year or so. With this three-song album, Mann changed the look and sound of jazz. A flute as the lead instrument --- extra points to anyone who can recall the last time that happened. A solid bass section. And rhythms that had as much to do with Brazil as Birdland. New. All new.

Someone wrote that there are only three "cool" jazz records from the late '50s and early '60s that you absolutely must have: "Kind of Blue" by Miles Davis, "Time Out" by Dave Brubeck, and Herbie Mann "At the Village Gate." Just so. ■

MUSIC

ROCK

JJ Cale

JJ Cale died on July 26th, 2013 at 74. If your interest in music is casual and anecdotal, you may know that Eric Clapton did not write "Cocaine" and "After Midnight" — Cale did. If you're a fan, you know more: J.J. Cale was a giant, a protean figure, bound for the pantheon — an immortal.

As a guitarist, Cale stands alongside Hendrix as an innovator. It's a funny pairing, for Cale was the exact opposite of Hendrix. His playing was quiet, minimal, in no way showy. It's not overstatement to suggest that Clapton owes him at least one of the last decades of his career. Mark Knopfler would admit he learned a thing or three from Cale. And there were others.

His guitar style was just the first reason to be awed by Cale. Another was his creative vision. He knew how he wanted his songs to sound, and he knew how to get them to sound that way. On many of his records he played all the instruments (with one exception: he used a drum machine) and sang backup. Then he mixed and produced the record. A one-man band, literally.

And then there is his writing. The titles suggest simplicity: "Call the Doctor," "Crazy Mama," "Don't Go to Strangers." But the songs are not at all simple — they defy categorization. Country, blues, jazz, shuffle, Okie rock: Cale's music cuts across genres. The common thread: you have to tap your feet. "He's good in a studio," a Tulsa friend said. "But you really want to hear him when he's playing on the back porch..."

Cale knew how good he was. But he was a laid-back guy who got a late start. He wasn't used to the spotlight, and the songwriting residuals were significant, so if he did not exactly run from the spotlight, he certainly retreated from it. (It wasn't until late in his career that he allowed his picture to be on the cover of his records.)

Over 35 years, there weren't many records. (A friend has said, "Cale is very busy being unbusy.")

At most, 50 live performances a year. (I once saw him perform with his gaze on a music stand. No music on it. Can you spell p-e-r-v-e-r-s-e?)

On the subject of a new CD: "I played with some of these guys 40 years ago and I tell you, I don't think there's anyone on this record who's under 60 years old." (That's not marketing.)

The bottom line: Cale was a cult favorite. Like Nick Drake. Or Jeff Buckley. The difference is that you forget he wrote those songs — but you can't forget those riffs and hooks.

A story: Cale was pleased when Clapton recorded "After Midnight" in 1970. His pal, producer Audie Ashworth, was more than pleased. "I phoned Cale," Ashworth recalled, "and I said, 'It might be time for you to make your move. Do an album.' I said, 'Get your songs together.' He said, 'I'll do a single.' I said, 'It's an album market.' He said, 'I don't have that many songs,' so I said, 'Write some.' Three or four months later he called me. He said, 'I got the songs.' He drove in. He was driving a Volkswagen this time. He came in with his dog. He played me all those songs."

Cale's blend of genres was like nothing else in music. Ditto his sense of privacy. He got booked on a tour with Stevie Winwood and Traffic. On his days off, he'd fly back to Tulsa.

You can hear how self-effacing he was in the way he recorded.

As Ashworth has noted, "Cale always wanted the voice mixed down. We'd be sitting at the board and both of us were trying to get our hands on the faders. He was always pulling back the fader on the vocal. He'd mix his voice back in the bed. He said it made you want to lean into the music instead of leaning back from it. It would pull people in. He had definite ideas about mixes."

Maybe that's not self-effacing. Because that's exactly what Chopin did. And you do lean in and lap up every note — of which, because Cale was very very smart, there are very very few.

A flawless career. No false moves. Working hard and making it look easy. There's no one else I could say this about: J.J. Cale was *totally* cool.■

LEONARD COHEN

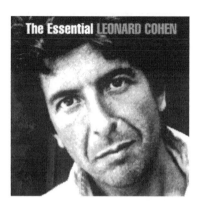
The Essential LEONARD COHEN

The backup singers sound like a parody of Motown. They chant, over and over, "In my secret life."And the singer's voice --- imagine a three-pack-a-day man at four in the morning with his dog recently dead.

His voice is a whispered croak, a tragic monotone. And this is what he declaims:

> *I smile when I'm angry.*
> *I cheat and I lie.*
> *I do what I have to do*
> *To get by.*
> *But I know what is wrong,*
> *And I know what is right.*
> *And I'd die for the truth*
> *In my secret life.*

Well, Leonard Cohen never said he made music for parties. He did say --- not in so many words, but this was the implicit promise --- that he'd stare the mirror down and make his secret life public. That he'd go "a thousand kisses deep" and report back. That, for the women who are his most passionate admirers, "I'm your man."

It's easy to see through Leonard Cohen --- at least that's what his critics say. To them, he's "the poet laureate of pessimism," "the grocer of despair," "the godfather of gloom," "the prince of bummers." His songs: "music to slit your wrists to."

His fans know different. I have been one since 1968, when I read his two novels and heard his first record. That album was like no other. It took itself seriously. And it took you seriously. That was the heart of the transaction --- a search for truth in a world where "even damnation is poisoned with rainbows" and God is always both present and mystifyingly silent.

That worldview sounds off-putting. Dark. Unrewarding. In fact, Cohen is --- for some of us --- immensely musical. Even inspiring. Or maybe that's the case when others perform or record his songs: Rufus Wainwright, Jeff Buckley, and, of course, Judy Collins.

Judy Collins, first. "Suzanne takes you down/to her boat by the river." That hit hap pened when Cohen started writing songs because he couldn't make a living as a novelist and thought --- quaintly --- that songwriting was the ticket. He called Collins one night and sang "Suzanne" through the phone. She knew its measure instantly and promptly recorded it. Later, at Carnegie Hall, she brought him onstage. Gaunt, poetic, handsome in a way that only some women appreciate, he stood there in his suit and shook. "I can't do this," he said, and rushed off.

But he could. He got a record contract with Columbia; he's now been with Columbia for almost four decades. Like Dylan. Like Springsteen. But with an ironic attitude about Columbia's concern for him: "I have always been touched by the modesty of their interest in my work."

Reviews? He's immune. Or, at the very least, sardonic: "I was born like this, I had no choice/I was born with the gift of a golden voice." The quest is the thing, always: "Like a bird on a wire/ Like a drunk in a midnight choir/ I have tried, in my way, to be free."

Early on, that quest led him to Zen Buddhism, the ideal choice for smarties who need to be quiet and listen. Cohen went further. He sought his teachers' advice on his music:

"Roshi came to the studio one night when I was recording 'New Skin for the Old Ceremony.' That was in the seventies. In those days I was being written off as a morbid old depressive drone peddling suicide notes. (Still am, in some circles). Roshi slept through most, but not all, of the session. The next morning I asked him what he thought. He said, 'Leonard, you should sing more sad.' That was the best advice I ever got. Took a while to put it into practice."

In recent years, that quest has taken him deeper --- he spent a decade in a Buddhist monastery, serving his teacher. He emerged in 2001 with "Ten New Songs." Of his recent work, it's a standout --- every song takes you under, wrings you out, shows you something new. And for a guy who has sometimes been content to stand on two or three chords, it's musically rich. Sadder? Hard to say.

If you are unfamiliar with Cohen and want to make a smart start --- well, that's a problem. Maybe his first record, "Songs of Leonard Cohen," because so much ambition is packed into that first, very accomplished album. Maybe, although I generally oppose anthologies, "The Essential Leonard Cohen."

Why is Cohen such a talisman for me? Because of the remarkable consistency of his vision. Others have detoured into politics, been fooled by chimera. Cohen, from the beginning, insisted on love as his topic. We're made in love. We disappear into love. We fail, often and gloriously. But the aspiration alone, however doomed, is triumphant. "There's a blaze of light/In every word."

Rufus Wainwright or Jeff Buckley --- you have heard them sing what, in the end, could be Cohen's signature song:

> *I did my best, it wasn't much*
> *I couldn't feel, so I tried to touch*
> *I've told the truth, I didn't come to fool you*
> *And even though*
> *It all went wrong*
> *I'll stand before the Lord of Song*
> *With nothing on my tongue but Hallelujah*

Not acceptance. Better: Hallelujah. But of course. "The holy or the broken Hallelujah" --- they're the same. In our imperfection lies our glory: "There's a crack in the world. That's how the light gets in."

Wherever you look, Cohen's been there. And moved on. To a place that looks almost exactly like the old one. Just a bit...brighter. Which, though odd, seems correct --- the king of bummers brightens the world. ■

Dr. John

I was in the right place, but it must have been the wrong time

I was sayin' the right things, but I must have used the wrong line

Anyone who can write those lines --- to say nothing of "What goes around, comes around" --- and set them to an irresistibly funky beat is not, shall we say, sitting in some suburb and drawing on poetic inspiration fueled by a drink you can buy at Starbucks.

This is knowledge that is hard won.

"Right time, wrong place" --- that's something you think around 3 AM, after you've poured Lord knows what down your throat and your money is gone and the women too.

Dr. John --- no one would mistake him for a healer in the traditional sense --- was born Mac Rebennack. He grew up in New Orleans, where music is in the blood at a tender age. School was not his thing. By 16, he was a working guitarist and, the books say, a heroin addict. Something went wrong, and he spent a season or two in jail. Something went wrong again --- a gun, a disagreement, the details are AWOL --- and he was shot in the hand, ending his career as a guitarist. But New Orleans was the right place, right time; he had cut his teeth on Fats Domino, Little Richard and Professor Longhair. The piano beckoned.

As did the particular charms of the mid-'60s. To New Orleans Creole lore, he added the spice of psychedelics. He wore Mardi Gras duds onstage. He invoked voodoo. Soon he was "Dr. John the Night Tripper."

Through the haze, I recall the first time I heard him. A good time was being had, and then someone put on "I Walk on Gilded Splinters" --- swamp music, with lyrics to match.

Over the top? Only a lot. This guy flew considerably higher than Mary Poppins. He was fun. And not shallow. "Refried confusion is making itself clear" --- those six words will speak to many survivors of an earlier time. And, with equal accuracy, to the present.■

Nick Drake

You remember the Volkswagen commercial. A moonlit night. A VW Cabriolet convertible. Two young couples driving along a lake road. Acoustic guitar music. The car reaches its destination: a club.

We see people coming in and out, sense the excitement and noise within. Close-up on the kids in the car: They'll skip the thrills of the club. And off they drive into the night.

The music was "Pink Moon," by Nick Drake.

It made him a star.

Alas, he had been dead for almost three decades.

There are musicians born for fame --- big-chested, thick-skinned, driven guys like Bruce and Bono --- and then there are musicians who just don't have the toughness for the game. Their music may be as good as that of the greats. But they drop by the wayside, and when they do, so does their music.

One of the goals of Head Butler is to find those artists --- and here, the word "artist" is apt --- and bring them to a community capable of appreciating them. Not that Nick Drake needs to be discovered. He's a cult. And has been, ever since he did or didn't kill himself in 1974 --- at age 26.

It's a sad story, and that, of course, is part of its attraction. Nick Drake was a riveting character --- six feet, three inches tall, with broad shoulders that he hunched up, like a turtle preparing to hide its head. He started playing guitar at an English boarding school, where, in the mid 1960s, he could not help but be influenced by the Beatles. He moved on to Cambridge University, where he was an indifferent student --- all he cared about was writing songs and perfecting them. At 20, a producer signed him to a recording contract, and he made "Five Leaves Left" --- the title comes from the warning message found near the end of packs of cigarette papers. It got great reviews. It didn't sell.

He made another CD. Same story. Crushed, he left London. When he returned, he brought with him "a black fog" that lasted for three years. A friend recalls: "He has a daily routine of sitting in a chair, gazing out of the window or staring at his feet. Sometimes he sits there in total darkness. He has by now moved back to his parents, but he is now and then driving to London. Sometimes he will change his mind half way there and drive back."

One night he decided he was ready to record again. He went into the studio and --- in two hours or two days; accounts differ --- made "Pink Moon." There were no arrangements, just his guitar and, on the title song, a piano. The album contained just 30 minutes of music, but that it exists at all is impressive; by this point, Drake was so withdrawn he could hardly speak.

"Pink Moon" suffered the same fate as its predecessors: great reviews, no sales. Drake returned to his parents' home, spent five weeks in a psychiatric hospital. Nothing worked: "I can't cope. All the defenses are gone, all the nerves are exposed." And then he overdosed on an anti-depressant. The coroner's verdict was suicide. But there was no note.

There's a boxed set of Drake's best songs, but it's built on a fallacy --- all his songs are his best. So start with "Five Leaves Left," his first CD, recorded when his career was still ahead of him and his sensitivity was leavened by flashes of hope:

> *Strange face, with your eyes*
> *So pale and sincere.*
> *Underneath you know well*
> *You have nothing to fear.*

There's an irony here. Nick Drake had no way to help himself, and yet his music helps us. Don't get caught up in that. Enormous pressure is put on coal, and, over time, we get diamonds. We can, if we like, remember how the coal suffered. But the diamonds --- how they shine. ∎

BOB DYLAN:
"JOHN WESLEY HARDING"

In 1967, a year when 11,153 body bags would come home, 467 arrived in the United States in October. That month, I went to Washington to protest; I watched peaceful people get beaten and arrested.

The culture was just as split. In greater America, "To Sir with Love" was the #1 song that month; in New York, "Hair" opened off-Broadway.

Bob Dylan? That month, he was in Nashville, recording a new album.

The first session, on October 17, lasted three hours; out of it came master takes of "I Dreamed I Saw St. Augustine," "Drifter's Escape" and "The Ballad of Frankie Lee and Judas Priest." On November 6, Dylan knocked off "All Along the Watchtower," "John Wesley Harding," "As I Went Out One Morning," "I Pity the Poor Immigrant" and "I Am a Lonesome Hobo." Late the next month, Dylan finished the album.

Twelve hours in the studio for 40 minutes of music --- there's no comparison in all of American music.

And that's just the start of What's Exceptional about "John Wesley Harding."

On December 27, 1967 --- a month after he finished recording, in the dead week between Christmas and New Year --- Columbia released the album. Promotion? None. A single? Not. Still, Dylan fans found it and snapped it up. And then it went away, until Jimi Hendrix plucked one song from it. "Two riders were approaching. The wind began to howl."

I can understand why "John Wesley Harding" may not be in your Dylan collection. It came after three of the greatest albums ever recorded: "Bringing It All Back Home," "Highway 61 Revisited" and "Blonde on Blonde." Then there was Dylan's motorcycle accident. And a long silence. And then this --- not quite a country album, though there were tendencies. With lyrics that teased and challenged: stripped-down story songs, vaguely Biblical in theme.

And not one word about Vietnam, drugs, hippies or the chasm between old and young.

I listened obsessively to "John Wesley Harding" that winter, and as the man says in one song, "I bowed my head and cried." First, for the artistic achievement; Dylan had, yet again, made something completely unexpected and contrarian. But even more for what I thought Dylan was saying. He'd taken a giant step back from everything contemporary and looked deeply into what mattered. What he found was scary, exhilarating, desperately important --- and absolutely relevant to what was happening.

Almost half a century later, I'm still listening to "John Wesley Harding." The reason is right at the start of the first song: "John Wesley Harding was a friend to the poor..." The whole album is shot through with references to losers: hoboes, immigrants, drifters. In short, everyone excluded from the national conversation right now. And then, even though you and I are still lucky enough to matter, the line we can all understand: "Dear landlord, please don't put a price on my soul."

If I make this sound heavy as German philosophy, I do my cause no favors here. The fact is, this is a fantastic listening experience, especially if you're listening through earphones. The band --- Charles McCoy (bass), Kenny Buttrey (drums) and Pete Drake (steel guitar) --- was amazed at Dylan's speed and self-assurance. Kenny Buttrey: "We went in and knocked 'em out like demos." True, but these were the best studio players in Nashville. And the producer was the legendary Bob Johnston.

And we are, after all, talking about our Shakespeare. ■

Levon Helm

LEVON HELM
DIRT FARMER

He's the one who sang "The Weight" and "The Night They Drove Old Dixie Down" and "Up on Cripple Creek." He's in rock's Hall of Fame. Rolling Stone called him one of the hundred best singers of all time.

Rock legends die all the time --- for some, death is how they become legends --- and the rituals of modern mourning follow. But losing Levon Helm felt different. He was one of the few Authentics, a dean of the Old School. As his wife and daughter say, "He loved nothing more than to play, to fill the room up with music, lay down the back beat, and make the people dance. He did it every time he took the stage."

Yes, he did. Back in pre-history, I saw The Band as often as I could. And in that hard, ugly time, I listened to The Band's records often, looking for a way to make sense of our country's twisted history. That sounds silly today; who looks now to a band for moral, spiritual or intellectual guidance? But those musicians had put in the time, and the care, and the living; they knew things. And the music was proof.

The custodian of The Band's music was Levon Helm, not Robbie Robertson. It could be no other way. There are jokes about drummers --- "Question: What does a drummer want to be when he grows up? Answer: A musician" --- but the truth is that the drummer is the literal heartbeat of a band. Levon was that, and more. Like Charlie Watts, he expanded the range of his instrument, freeing his partners from the lockstep of the rock beat.

Just by virtue of its name, The Band announced its mission was harmony and collaboration. That ambition was not universally shared. As critic Dave Marsh wrote, after seeing The Band's concert film, "Robbie Robertson demonstrated that he is one of the few people capable of making Bob Dylan seem humble."

For all Robertson's genius as a songwriter, the one you remember was Levon. Maybe only insiders grasped the subtleties of his drumming. But when he sang, you knew who you were hearing.

"Virgil Caine is the name, and I served on the Danville train."

"When I get off of this mountain, you know where I want to go..."

"I pulled into Nazareth, I was feelin' about half past dead."

He came from the country, he was those men. Born the son of a cotton farmer and sometime musician in Turkey Scratch, Arkansas, he sounded as if he never got further north than Little Rock. His high-lonesome voice held the howl of the poor farmer and his cousin, the coal miner --- it's pure Americana, mesmerizing in 1967, mesmerizing forever, but unlikely to be played now on any radio station not run by a college. That voice is the direct route to an America that was about taking care of your family, Saturday night frolic and an abiding faith that there was glory on the other side of life's wide, wide river.

His path was destined. At 6, he heard Bill Monroe and His Blue Grass Boys; at 9, he got a guitar; by 12, he and his sister were winning 4-H Club talent contests. At 15, he saw Elvis and was struck by the power of his band; he took up drums, and, at 17, found himself playing with Ronnie Hawkins.

And then, in his early 20s, he teamed up with four Canadians --- Richard Manuel, Rick Danko, Robbie Robertson and Garth Hudson. The Hawks, as they were known, played music that had pounding American rock at its heart. But it was a very roomy heart --- it also contained country, mountain-tinged bluegrass, the 19th century sound of Stephen Foster, folk and blues.

When Bob Dylan went electric, he chose The Hawks as his backup band. Controversy followed, then history. The Hawks became The Band, and, at the height of the Vietnam War, five bearded men who looked as if they'd stepped out of a Matthew Brady photograph made a generation of heartsick Americans forget all about acid rock.

Fame came. It was no barrier against Real Life. In 1986, while Helm was in a hotel room down the hall, Richard Manuel committed suicide. In 1991, a fire ravaged Helm's home and studio in Woodstock, New York. In 1999, Rick Danko died in his sleep.

The bad news turned lethal for Levon Helm, a three-pack-a-day smoker. He was diagnosed with throat cancer; he couldn't speak for years. Chemo killed the disease; his voice was collateral damage. So were his finances. Caught between competing bills, he decided to pay his doctors instead of his mortgage. Inevitably, he was threatened with the loss of his home.

I can't confirm this story, but it sounds right: Bruce Springsteen showed up with a check for $1 million. Levon thanked him, said he couldn't accept it, and began the "Midnight Rambles" concert series in his barn, singing with his daughter Amy. The Rambles began attracting audiences --- and musical legends --- and soon commanded $200 a ticket. There was even a guy in a field waving a flashlight to show you where to park; naturally, he was "Helmland Security."

The Rambles led him back to recording. "Dirt Farmer" sounds as if it's barn music, as if Levon Helm is a senior citizen who has just come in from the fields and would like to sit on the porch and have a chew, but has been dragooned to play some tunes. Be not fooled. It may feature songs that Helm grew up on and songs from modern masters --- Steve Earle, Buddy and Julie Miller --- that feel just as sepia-toned, but the hand-made metaphors end right there. "Dirt Farmer" is not just entertainment; it's art, worthy of close listening and deep meditation, superficially simple but musically sophisticated, easily one of the greater releases of 2007.

His revival continued. He made a terrific live album in Nashville, "Ramble at the Ryman." He won a Grammy. Did he know he lived under a shadow? Certainly. You don't record "Wide River to Cross" for laughs. But it's "When I Go Away" that sums up the man and his work:

> Early in the morning
> When the church bells toll
> The choir's gonna sing
> And the hearse will roll
> On down to the graveyard
> Where it's cold and gray
> And then the sun's gonna shine
> Through the shadows
> When I go away
>
> Don't want no sorrow
> For this old orphan boy
> I don't want no crying
> Only tears of joy
> I'm gonna see my mother
> Gonna see my father
> And I'll be bound for glory
> In the morning
> When I go away
>
> I'll be lifted up to the clouds
> On the wings of angels
> There's only flesh and bones
> In the ground
> Where my troubles will stay
> See that storm over yonder
> It's gonna rain all day
> But then the sun's gonna shine
> Through the shadows
> When I go away

In the liner notes of one of his records, he wrote: "I love you all for giving us a fair hearing."

Love you back. ∎

LOVE

Beware the aging boomer come to tell you about a neglected masterpiece from the 1960s, an album so great it stands with the best of the Beatles. Pity his failing eyesight, his muddied hearing. And ignore him.

The thing is, there is such an album, and it is that good, and people who have the history of rock music in their heads put it in the pantheon. The group is Love. They made a few albums, and then, in 1968, they made "Forever Changes." Arthur Lee --- the leader of Love --- thought it was his swan song; he expected his imminent death.

"Forever Changes" was huge in the band's native Los Angeles, big on a few campuses, ignored everywhere else. And not because of the songs: they are smartly written and expertly played. But they are also "produced" --- there are strings here, and horns. In a summer when police were beating kids at the Democratic Convention in Chicago and we were dropping more bombs on Vietnam than we did in World War II and Bobby Kennedy and Martin Luther King, Jr. were getting killed, the last thing Young America wanted was Smart and Complex.

Time clarifies. Dust settles. Now no one cares who did what back when. Without expectations, maybe you can actually hear this CD for what it is.

What you'll hear is a blend of rock and psychedelia.

There's the punch of rock lyrics --- "The news today will be the movies for tomorrow" ---- and the longing of high-altitude, late-night musing:

> *Yeah, I heard a funny thing*
> *Somebody said to me*
> *You know that I could be in love with almost everyone*
> *I think that people are*
> *The greatest fun*
> *And I will be alone again tonight my dear*

Or this:

> *You are just a thought that someone*
> *Somewhere somehow feels you should be here*
> *And it's so for real*
> *To touch, to smell, to feel, to know where you are here*
> *And the streets are paved with gold*
> *And if someone asks you, you can call my name*

For all the romanticism, there's plenty of paranoia. Lee recites, over martial drums:

> *They're locking them up today*
> *they're throwing away the key*
> *I wonder who it will be tomorrow*
> *--- you or me?*

But in this song cycle about confusion and thwarted romance and the deep ache for wholeness, there's a surprisingly upbeat conclusion:

> *This is the time and life that I am living*
> *And I'll face each day with a smile*
> *For the time that I've been given is such a little while*
> *And the things that I must do consist of more than style*

At the end, Arthur Lee invokes the idea contained in the title:

> *Everything I've seen needs rearranging*
> *And for anyone who thinks it's strange*
> *Then you should be the first to want to make this change*
> *And for everyone who thinks that life is just a game*
> *Do you like the part you're playing?*

Love didn't. The group broke up. Arthur Lee spent more than a decade in jail for a gun violation. And died. And now here is "Forever Changes," re-mixed, even better, fresh as a spring morning in Los Angeles decades and decades ago. Oh, dear. That long? ■

Joni Mitchell: "Blue"

A few years after she recorded "Blue," Joni Mitchell came to one of my parties. She was a pleasure to chat with --- I was not a fan, and so was not struck dumb by her unexpected appearance.

What? Not a fan? My Lord, Joni Mitchell was *huge* back then. *Everybody* listened to her! *Everybody* revered her!

No. "Everybody" didn't. Women did. All the women in my circle, anyway. They loved Mitchell's trilly voice, naked lyrics, insistence on independence, her secondary gift as a painter --- for them, Joni Mitchell was a role model.

Maybe I was threatened by such a gifted woman, by such a quicksilver spirit. Maybe I suspected that women who operated out of honesty and innocence were beyond me. What man would willingly look into a light that bright? Not many. Not me, anyway.

But you know how it goes. Life beats you up. And, eventually, the wind tunnel of experience knocks off your slick charm and easy certainty. And then an album that "everyone" was listening to in 1971 makes its way to your ears --- 30 or 40 years late.

Not that the road to "Blue" was easy for Joni Mitchell. By 1970, she was weary of touring and recording and the life of the rising star. So she "retired," the better to write: "I have to go inside myself so far, to search through a theme." Ten songs later, she was ready to record.

There's a limited palette in "Blue," but it's the kind you want: "At that period of my life, I had no personal defenses, so there's hardly a dishonest note in the vocals." The instrumentation is in the same flavor: scarce. James Taylor. Stephen Stills. A few others. Which leaves the words --- and the singer-songwriter --- totally exposed.

There's one song with news in it. When young and unknown, she had a daughter, and she doesn't sugarcoat her reaction to giving the child up for adoption: "You sign all the papers in the family name/ You're sad and you're sorry but you're not ashamed." The rest of the songs are about the men she met, mostly on her travels in Europe. They're dashing and romantic and verbally acute --- and she is as much of a trial to them as they are to her: "I'm so hard to handle, I'm selfish and I'm sad."

These songs are love letters, of the greediest, most voluptuous kind. "I could drink a case of you," she sings. "I want to be the one that you want to see." But she's restless, always moving on: "I'm going to make a lot of money/ Then I'm going to quit this crazy scene/ I wish I had a river I could skate away on."

"Blue" is a CD that's cherished by many. It may bring up memories of your own failed romances, but that kind of discomfort is good for you. Good for me, anyway. The spirit that created "Blue" is gifted and frightened, dangerous and alive --- and fresh. Eternally fresh.

Time is kind to art that aims for so much, and hits the mark. ∎

Van Morrison: "Astral Weeks"

In 1968, I lived in Cambridge, Massachusetts, just down the block from Van Morrison. Whenever we passed one another on the street, I would nod. Morrison would stare. Or glare. "Unpleasant," I concluded.

I have seen Van Morrison in concert many times over the past 40-odd years. I have never had to reconsider this opinion. Van Morrison is one chilly, angry guy.

But we shouldn't judge artists on personality, only their work. And so the important thing to know is that, in 1968, Morrison went to New York, and, in just two or three days and for a total cost of about $22,000, recorded "Astral Weeks."

For a record that's #19 on the Rolling Stone list of all-time greats, "Astral Weeks" seems under-appreciated. On classic rock and alternative radio alike, I rarely hear it. Over the years, I have bought it for dozens of people, many of them Morrison fans, and very few seemed to know of its existence.

Clearly, "Astral Weeks" is no "Moondance."

What it is is much harder to say. It's a song cycle that's jazzy, tormented, light years from the psychedelia that dominated rock music in 1968. It's a visionary meditation that's both timeless and prescient ("Madame George" is the first song I ever heard about a drag queen). And then it's a mystical space shot hurled aloft on butterfly wings (the backup musicians are an acoustic guitarist, acoustic bassist, a subliminal drummer, a flutist and, from time to time, a string quartet) and anchored by a voice that starts in Ireland, transits to Mississippi and ultimately resides in that place called Genius.

And the writing! This is how the record starts:

> *If I ventured in the slipstream*
> *Between the viaducts of your dreams*
> *Where the mobile steel rims crack*
> *And the ditch and the back roads stop*
> *Could you find me*
> *Would you kiss my eyes*
> *And lay me down*
> *In silence easy*
> *To be born again*

The great rock critic Lester Bangs wrote reams in praise of "Astral Weeks," but this passage sums it up:

Van Morrison was twenty-two --- or twenty-three --- years old when he made this record; there are lifetimes behind it. What "Astral Weeks" deals in are not facts but truths. "Astral Weeks," insofar as it can be pinned down, is a record about people stunned by life, completely overwhelmed, stalled in their skins, their ages and selves, paralyzed by the enormity of what in one moment of vision they can comprehend.

You can play it as background music; it's that pretty. But if you listen to it --- really listen to it --- you will find yourself being taken deep inside, to the part of you that, I suspect, you care about most: the part where the only thing that matters is what happens between you and one other person. Though it may be quiet in there, it's far from peaceful; this is where we conduct the epic battle between self and surrender, between risk and loneliness.

It's a very personal piece of music; this is just how it seems to me. I'm now on my fifth or sixth copy. And decades after the fact, I still believe that if you give "Astral Weeks" a chance, you will play it as long as you live. ∎

JOSH RITTER:
"THE BEAST IN ITS TRACKS"

I love silent days crafting sentences alone, but if you put a gun to my head and told me I'd have to work on the stages of music clubs and receive universal critical praise... yeah, I guess I could stand being Josh Ritter.

From his first release, a decade ago, to "The Beast in Its Tracks," this guy hasn't made a foolish move. As a writer, he produces lyrics that, if they were prose, you'd underline them. As a singer, he's like Leonard Cohen, Nick Drake, Paul Simon; there's one person he's trying to reach, and that's you. And in performance, backed by a crackerjack band, he's mesmerizing: exuberant, goofy, unfiltered and absolutely delighted to be onstage. No one has ever had more fun at a Josh Ritter concert than Josh Ritter.

This time, newcomers will find an exploration of darker themes. "The Beast in Its Tracks" is a "breakup" record --- his version of Dylan's "Blood on the Tracks" --- because he wrote these songs in response to his wife's out-of-the-blue announcement that, after just a year, their marriage was over. I understand this shorthand, but I don't think it will last long. I see "Beast" as his "breakthrough" record.

For a writer who can toss off long, convoluted lyrics, he's served up 13 fairly simple songs here. And they're surprisingly jolly --- he's not cranking up the band for take that, bitch revenge songs. He's got a new lover; he hopes his ex-wife does too. (He hasn't totally forsaken clever; in that song's final line, he notes that if she's still alone, "well, that would make me happy too.") His new lover is "hopeful" for him. He's thrilled to be "in your arms again."

For the English majors in his fan base, some of these songs may seem like throwaways. For the English majors in his fan base, some of these songs may seem like throwaways. Not so. Their strength is in their simplicity, their directness, their universality. We've all been shattered by the disappearance of love, and it's not a feeling you forget. But being lost and getting found and the sheer joy of feeling free to risk love again and having that courage rewarded --- who wouldn't go to school on that? Best to say it straight: simple statement, upbeat music. The songs in "Beast" are like early Beatles songs; the appeal is in the sound, not the words.

It wouldn't be a Josh Ritter CD if it didn't have at least one song that's all over FM radio. Here that song is "Joy to You Baby." It's got an irresistible melody that lodges in your head and won't leave. And it has a generosity of spirit that's unprecedented in modern pop music. Remember: these lyrics are directed to his ex-wife:

joy to the city/ joy to the streets/ and joy to you baby wherever
you sleep/ tonight tonight tonight

so joy to the many/ joy to the few/ joy to you baby/
and joy to me too/ tonight tonight tonight

A few words about the ending....

There's pain in whatever, we stumbled upon
If I never had met you, you couldn't have gone
But then I wouldn't have met you, we couldn't have been
I guess it all adds up to joy in the end...

You can boil that down to "It's all good" --- a pop songwriter probably would. But this is a little more exalted; it evokes Mindfulness 101, basic Buddhism. It's a hymn to aliveness, a gentle reminder that, somehow, we got here. We're here now. Here we are. And it's all good. ∎

Roxy Music: "Avalon"

Mortally wounded, King Arthur was brought to the enchanted island of Avalon and placed on a golden bed. Enchanted, indeed --- the island was always ruled by a woman, and all her followers were women.

On the cover photo of "Avalon," the final album released by Roxy Music, we see the back of a knight's helmet. Resting on his hand is a falcon. They look out over clouds and what seems like the rising sun to a strip of land in the distance --- a goal so prized it might as well be Avalon, the paradise where the knight could find rest. And comfort. Even, perhaps, love.

The power of women to heal --- it's the link between the myth and this CD. Bryan Ferry was always a ladies man, that is, a man who lived for love. The dark suit, the white shirt, the hair cut just so across the forehead. It's all atmosphere, all sensuality. The rhythm that redefined "sultry." The ethereal saxophone. The elliptical lyrics that conjured, all at once, rainy nights on Fifth Avenue, women beautiful as models, champagne served on penthouse terraces, the lucidity that strikes at 4 AM when the party's finally over.

But let's be clear --- this is no virginal search for first love, there are no teenagers here. In the world that Roxy Music evokes, the narrator knows so much about love he's jaded. Been there, done that, got the heartache to prove it. And yet he's still a romantic.

So the first thing to say about "Avalon" is that this music is sexy sexy sexy. Indeed, if you were trying to explain sex to an alien and could only use sound, this is the CD you'd play; in essence, it is sex. Not wholehearted Barry White sex. Not popper-fueled KC and the Sunshine Band sex. But slow, dreamy sex; deep, underwater sex; dark, midnight sex. Above all, sex so powerful it passes for love, sex that might as well be love.

No wonder "Avalon" has been so popular as "first time" background music --- this is music that respects, even exalts, women. (On the Amazon page for "Avalon," a man writes that "Any, and I mean any, guy going to college during the early to mid eighties understands the importance of this record/CD in regards to taking care of business with their girlfriends.")

"Avalon" presents ten tracks (two of them instrumentals), a grand total of 35 minutes of music --- and stripped-to-the-bone music at that. The sax, bass and percussion are extraordinary, but the emphasis is on the keyboards and Bryan Ferry's world-weary ("Who cares about you/ Except me, God help me/ When things go wrong") quest. And the lyrics --- they're all sketches, suggestions of pictures, allowing you (or even encouraging you) to fill in the blanks. As, for example, over a languid samba melody:

> *Now the party's over*
> *I'm so tired*
> *Then I see you coming*
> *Out of nowhere*
> *Much communication in a motion*
> *Without conversation or a notion*

"Avalon" defies genre. In its effort to describe the ideal, it becomes the ideal --- an object of beauty, a piece of art. If anything, it has improved since its 1982 release; a re-mix a few years ago makes it sound even more pristine, unadorned, exquisite in its nakedness.

Music is transportation; it takes you somewhere. "Avalon" takes you --- takes me, anyway --- somewhere at once long ago and right now, somewhere distant and intimate. As such, it inspires us --- well, me, anyway --- to aim higher and feel more deeply. And, of course, to manifest love. ∎

TEDDY THOMPSON

The line on Teddy Thompson is that he's just too fantastic for his own good. Too gifted a writer, too compelling a singer, too handsome a man. And too insistently artistic to release a CD of songs that kids want to buy.

It's a damn shame. Who can save Teddy Thompson? Really smart women. Why do I think this? Personal experience.

My veddy British trainer screamed like a schoolgirl when Teddy stepped on stage.

After a few songs, my friend Gretl said, "I want to grab him and pull on his hair."

Women over 25 --- he's catnip to them.

Maybe Vogue could do a think piece on his winsome combination of good cheer and self-loathing. Or, because he can look like England's Prince William when he's shaved and cleaned up, he could model for Ralph Lauren. And then Teddy might get TV producers interested in mining his CDs for songs --- and there are many --- that would hold female viewers at the end of a TV drama. Next stop: stardom.

Has the promotion of Teddy Thompson really come to gimmicks? I resist that conclusion, though, clearly, the exquisite quality of his music has failed to work much magic.

Let's try a different tack --- a charm offensive.

Now "charm" may not be the first word that comes to mind when you're talking about Teddy Thompson. Yes, he's in love with love; he wants it badly.

But he's also a toxic lover, who sings "I was born with a love disease/ It's known as chronic hard to please" and "Forward me to someone new" and "I'm looking for a girl who's easy on the eye/ But not so fucking stupid she makes me want to cry."

On the other hand, he's funny and ironic and self-aware, good qualities all. So let's just... chat with Teddy Thompson.

Two things fascinate me about him. One is artistic: how he came to write some of the most intimate lyrics this side of Leonard Cohen. And second, how those songs play out in the real world --- in his relationships with women. Thinking of my Teddy-intoxicated female friends, I started our conversation there.

JK: Do women see you as a challenge --- the Everest of men?

TT: Most women I date don't know who I am... I'm not famous enough. I meet women in bars and parties.

JK: But isn't there a recognition moment: "You're the guy in those songs!"

TT: Never happens. Anyway, they're already involved with me before they find out.

JK: Do you ever get this reaction from women who like you: "Teddy, I'm hooked on your music, and I think I could help you."

TT: In the beginning, it's not about music.

JK: Eventually, they come to your show. Is that disarming?

TT: Only when they say: I'm more into techno.

JK: Later, though, your songs suggest that your relationships always sour.

TT: Then they see that some of the songs are true.

JK: In what way?

TT: I like to be on my own a lot.

JK: How much time can you spend alone before you feel, as your song has it, "I must get up/ I must go out/ There must be something/ I can't do without?"

TT: A week.

JK: During that week, what do you do?

TT: Stay home. Listen to music. Watch TV. I pretty much prefer people in short spurts. Here's my worst nightmare: You meet someone for lunch. They say: "Let's do something after." Then they say: "Coffee?" And it goes on all day...

JK: Maybe it would be better if you were romantically involved with a musician.

TT: Never done it. Might have ego trouble.

JK: Do you "need" to write?

TT: I finish nothing without a deadline.

JK: Isn't that the real mark of a professional? Don't people who have nothing to say say it all the time?

TT: You know the Chuck Berry story? He got a call: "Come in and cut a record." He got on a train with 3 songs. He got off the train with 7 more. His biggest hits, in fact.

JK: How quickly have you written a song?

TT: A day. I play guitar all the time. That's recreation --- it doesn't seem like work. When I have to record, I have to finish things.

JK: Where are your parents [the legendary English guitarist Richard Thompson and his ex-wife, the folk-rock singer Linda Thompson] as examples or influences?

TT: They were just encouraging enough. Which was right on the money.

JK: I saw you do a terrific show. After, you were hard on yourself. What happens when you go home?

TT: After a show that disappoints me, I have the urge to come home and practice. But usually I just crumble. Fall into bed. Get depressed. Then try to regroup.

JK: Therapy?

TT: Tried it. Useful. Stopped when I went on tour.

JK: Now that no one sells CDs, touring is where you make your living. But I'm not convinced you like performing all that much.

TT: I like touring for all that goes with it. Hanging out with friends, drinking in bars, hotels, the guys. It's what they say: "Aren't we having fun --- if only we didn't have to do the gig!" The thing is, I do enjoy performing --- when it's right.

JK: How often is that?

TT: One in three is great. One in three is ok. And one is terrible.

JK: Define "right."

TT: Very little to do with me. It's the audience and the room. It's the sound guy, the sound of the band. When I'm alone, it's easier. Add a band, it's all up in the air.

JK: Would it be easier if your ad libs were less spontaneous?

TT: I love not knowing what to say each night. That's the upside. Even if 20% is on the edge of great or terrible, that's exciting to me. I'm a confidence player, as they say in sports. I'm not the steady fullback who always comes through for you.

JK: Was it was easier when you played in someone else's band?

TT: Like with Rosanne Cash? Yes. It's fun to be in someone's band --- freeing. It's all the things I normally do... with no one looking at me. Then after a while, you go: "Could someone look at me?" Ultimately, music for me is a way to write songs for me to play.

JK: In your writing, I hear outrageous variety --- '50s rock, classic country, power pop --- and there's more.

TT: Well, I don't quite know who I want to be. There are so many styles I like. My friend Rufus [Wainwright] is totally distinctive --- he knows who he is and what he does well. On the way to the studio, he won't hear a country song and think, "Oh, I want to do that." I do. It's not a bad thing.

JK: Do you mind that your music makes listeners think: Those songs --- they're all about Teddy?

TT: It is all about me. I know it sounds egotistical, but it's the only way I know how to do it.

JK: Flaubert cried when he wrote the death of Madame Bovary. Do you get excited when you write a great line?

TT: No. I tend to think something is good later. When I'm writing, I'm just struggling to fill in the gaps.

JK: Do you save good lines in notebooks other songwriters might want to steal?

TT: It's all in my head. Sometimes I sing into my computer. But my songwriting philosophy is: survival of the fittest.

JK: Do you read reviews?

TT: I wish I could say I didn't. But people send them to you. Or you can't resist Google. When it's negative, I generally think: They have a point.

Final thought: No. They don't. Good is good. Better is better. Teddy Thompson is just great. ■

THE TRAVELING WILBURYS

George Harrison had been in a band. He wasn't looking to start another. But in 1988 he had a solo CD coming out. He had a song that could be a hit single. He needed another song --- a new song, a song not on the CD --- as its "B-side."

Back then, Harrison was living in Los Angeles and hanging out with Bob Dylan. And Tom Petty. And Jeff Lynne (once of Electric Light Orchestra). And Roy Orbison, the most distinctive singer in all of rock and roll.

As Harrison dashed off a song, he got an idea: "I thought, 'I'm not gonna just sing it myself, I've got Roy Orbison standing there -- I'm gonna write a bit for Roy to sing.' And then as it progressed, I thought I might as well push it a bit and get Tom and Bob to sing the bridge."

Would this crew sing with George Harrison? In a heartbeat. The very next day, Dylan was toying with the lyrics and Orbison was wailing, "I'm so tired of being lonely/I still have some love to give," and Harrison was serving up a gorgeous guitar figure. Ooops. The song had no title. Someone saw a sticker on a carton: Handle with Care. And, just like that, it was done.

But there was a problem: "Handle with Care" was too good --- too bouncy, catchy, joyous --- to languish as the flip side of a single. It had come so easily; maybe there was more where that came from. A band with four acoustic guitarists --- with four superstar guitarists who had no urgent need to be in a band? There was something egoless and attractive about the idea. So George Harrison asked his friends. No one turned him down.

Dylan was about to go on one of his endless tours; the songs for the CD needed to be written and recorded in about two weeks. A song a day, every day, for 14 days. In the dictionary, that's one definition of "impossible" --- for in addition to the songs, the band lacked a studio and a name.

Harrison settled on the house of a friend who had a mixing deck and a kitchen large enough to double as a studio. The origin of the band's name is lost in a fog of joints and beer, but it seems to have something to do with the idea of mistakes being fixed later, as "We'll bury it in the mix." That morphed to Trembling Wilburys, then Traveling Wilburys, with its suggestion of a clan of itinerant musicians.

"Traveling Wilburys Volume 1" sold five million copies. Roy Orbison died a month after it went on sale. Though he was irreplaceable, the band soldiered on, releasing a highly regarded second CD: "Traveling Wilburys Volume 3."

The songs are easy-going rock, with more humor than profundity. Like this, from Dylan:

> *You don't need no wax job*
> *You're smooth enough for me*
> *If you need your oil changed*
> *I'll do it for you --- free*

And this, from a novelty dance number called "The Wilbury Twist":

> *Turn your lights down low*
> *Put your blindfold on*
> *You'll never know*
> *Where your friends have gone*

But the real pleasure is in the harmonies. No music is sweeter to me than voices blending together to make something finer than any individual voice could create. And that is totally the case here. It's the coolest thing --- Harrison set it up so almost every song has a rotating set of solos, but it's the collective experience you take away. And I'm not talking about just music here. These are friends celebrating their friendship. There's a sweetness about that you almost never see.

Because these CDs feel like professional music made for private pleasure, it's nice that the two-CD set also has a DVD. On it, you'll find the band's videos, as well as footage from 1988. It's riveting to watch Dylan write and record, it's fascinating to hear the Wilburys talk about one another --- hell, it's a hoot just to watch these guys hang out.

Time changes everything. Orbison gone. Harrison gone. For a package that's nothing but fun, you can't help but get a lump in the throat when rich and famous musicians leave all that behind and connect with the least of us:

> *Don't have to be ashamed of the car I drive*
> *I'm just glad to be here, happy to be alive* ∎

IKE AND TINA TURNER

"River Deep Mountain High" --- the song ranked #33 on Rolling Stone's list of "500 Best Songs of All Time" --- is credited to Ike & Tina Turner. But it's 100% Phil Spector.

For those who aren't of a certain age, some explanation is in order. Ike Turner? Who he? And Phil Spector --- isn't he the LA freak who killed a woman?

Gather round, kids, and let me tell you a story. It's about one song...

Phil Spector loved mono. Hated stereo. Thought it was an artificial way to chop music into parts. Indeed, the whole and entire point of rock 'n roll was to sound great on a car radio. Over a tiny speaker. And the way to do that was to make the music a fist --- a unified wave of instrumentation and voice that hits the listener right in the face. This was the "Wall of Sound," and it was Spector's signature.

In 1966, Ike & Tina Turner were a touring act. Ike was a monomaniac; he was the star, Tina was the add-on. (Indeed, she had only been Ike's lead singer for four years, and then only because Ike's favorite female vocalist failed to show up at a recording session.) There are stories that Ike beat Tina --- who knows what's true?

But in 1966, Spector had a vision, and he had Jeff Barry and Ellie Greenwich --- who had written "Da Doo Ron Ron" and "Be My Baby" --- write "River Deep Mountain High" for Tina Turner. The song was, Spector thought, destined to be his masterpiece.

Here, for those who have not heard it, are the lyrics:

When I was a little girl I had a rag doll
The only doll I've ever owned
Now I love you just the way I loved that rag doll
But only now my love has grown
And it gets stronger in every way
And it gets deeper let me say
And it gets higher day by day
Do I love you my oh my
River deep, mountain high
If I lost you would I cry
Oh how I love you baby, baby, baby, baby

When you were a young boy did you have a puppy
That always followed you around
Well I'm gonna be as faithful as that puppy
No I'll never let you down

Cause it goes on and on like a river flows
And it gets bigger baby and heaven knows
And it gets sweeter baby as it grows
Do I love you my oh my
River deep, mountain high

Clearly, those silly lyrics were not what the song was about. The sound was everything, and so you have to imagine Tina Turner screaming the refrain --- it is said the recording session was so sweaty for her that she finished the recording in her underwear --- over music that was operatic in its dimensions. The ultimate marriage of R&B and rock. Meant to be played LOUD. In mono. Wagnerian. Massive. So totally overwhelming that listeners would have no choice but to jump to their feet, fling themselves about and go limp when it ended.

Spector, who hadn't had a hit for eighteen months, was obsessed with the production of this one song --- for about six months. It was going to be his masterpiece. Some thought it was. George Harrison called it a perfect record. Brian Wilson was floored. But the kids had moved on. "River Deep Mountain High" was a hit in England --- and a total flop in America.

Why did the song fail? Here is Dave Marsh: "The song is mediocre, the lyric absurd; the production is more bombastic than millennial, and in Tina Turner, a harsh, adult blues singer, Spector encountered the most inappropriate object of his production style."

Those words were written decades ago. Doubtful that Marsh would write them today. For "River Deep Mountain High" has taken its place in music history --- mad, everything-on-the-table sound that's like nothing else in rock or soul. As Spector said a few years after its release, "I just wanted to go crazy for four minutes on wax."

There are eleven other songs on this CD, all of them first rate. A bunch of singles, taken together, do make an album --- and a classic. Insane that it hasn't been re-released by an American label. Wonderful that it is, however, available as an import.

"River Deep Mountain High" --- to know it is to love it. ∎

WARREN ZEVON

Unless you're hard-core, what you know about Warren Zevon is that he wrote "Werewolves of London" and some song that had the line "send lawyers, guns and money," and that he contracted an incurable form of cancer and died.

Or you know his name because there was a tribute CD out that featured Bruce Springsteen, Bob Dylan, Jackson Browne, Don Henley and many more on it.

Why, you may wonder, were they so fond of this Los Angeles-based singer-songwriter?

Well, he was charming. Witty. Ironic. Self-deprecating. Not qualities often associated with rock stars. But then, Zevon was the son of a minor Los Angeles gangster; he knew his way around.

More to the point, he was talented. Across the board, and at the highest level. He wrote great lyrics. He wrote great music. He was The Compleat Package. The bookend, in 1976, to Jackson Browne.

And it is to 1976 that we turn, on the theory that first releases are often the best releases --- the purest expressions of talent and ambition.

Certainly that was true of Warren Zevon's first, self-titled CD. It's got ambition all over it. Jackson Browne was the producer. Stevie Nicks and Bonnie Raitt and Don Henley and Phil Everly sang on it. The musicians are on the order of Lindsay Buckingham and Glenn Frey. Linda Ronstadt would get hit after hit from this collection.

There are eleven songs on this CD. Most are love songs, though the love is bent all out of shape.

As here:

> *She's so many women*
> *He can't find the one who was his friend*
> *So he's hanging on to half her heart*
> *He can't have the restless part*
> *So he tells her to hasten down the wind*

And here:

> *Well, I met a girl in West Hollywood*
> *I ain't naming names*
> *She really worked me over good*
> *She was just like Jesse James*
> *She really worked me over good*
> *She was a credit to her gender*

Naturally, the man who endures these women has what might be called a tragic viewpoint:

> *I'd lay my head on the railroad tracks*
> *And wait for the Double "E"*
> *But the railroad don't run no more*
> *Poor, poor pitiful me*

That drunk/stoned take on life extends even to the last song, a serious meditation on the end of California as we know it.

> *Don't the sun look angry through the trees*
> *Don't the trees look like crucified thieves*
> *Don't you feel like desperados under the eaves*
> *Heaven help the one who leaves*
>
> *Still waking up in the mornings with shaking hands*
> *And I'm trying to find a girl who understands me*
> *But except in dreams you're never really free*
> *Don't the sun look angry at me*
>
> *I was sitting in the Hollywood Hawaiian Hotel*
> *I was listening to the air conditioner hum*
> *It went mmmmmm.*

And then there's a gospel choir, singing "Look away..." But if you listen closely, they're singing "Look away down Gower Avenue..." --- that beautiful choral sound is an invitation to look down a grotty Los Angeles Street. You feel the inspiration and get the humor all at once; emotions wash together, and you realize you're in the presence of a presence.

Warren Zevon knew that a little sincerity goes a long way. In this CD, made before fame pushed his tongue further into his cheek, he had just the right amount. He'd go on to make other, bigger-selling CDs, but this one's the keeper, the desert island disk, the reason to wish he was still here. ∎

MUSIC

SOUL

Otis Redding

One of the greatest live recordings ever made begins with the corniest of intro-ductions --- a self-consciously "groovy" MC has the French audience spell out the star's name. I cringed. You will too.

But all's forgiven when the bass player delivers eight throbbing notes, as elemental and indelible as the opening to "Satisfaction." Here comes the trumpet, playing tight little circles. And a drummer who'd rather pound on tom-toms than keep time on snares. And then here is Otis Redding, gripping a hand mike and taking one last deep breath.

And out comes... "Respect." This song was so powerfully covered by Aretha Frank-lin that it's easy to think she wrote it, that's it's a woman's plea, but the trick of this song --- in fact, the brilliance of so much of Otis Redding's music --- is the universal-ity of need.

Do you regard male vulnerability as first cousin to weakness?

Do you believe that big boys don't cry?

Otis Redding is the proof that machismo has nothing to do with masculinity, that the sensitive guy gets the girl. Otis is, without question, all man; Otis is, without peer, all emotion. And so his version of the best song he ever wrote delivers an ur-gent double declaration to his lover: I have love to give, but I also need love. (Pride? Not here. He goes so far as to give her permission to cheat: "Do me wrong/while you're gone.")

But the words almost don't matter. Otis Redding's genius was in his voice, easily the most distinctive in the history of soul music. "Rasp" doesn't begin to convey how rough it was. Imagine someone who's been yelling for hours, whose vocal cords are so ragged he should really be home drinking tea and honey. Instead, he goes on stage and shouts out his songs until he reaches a pitch so desperate he dispenses with lyrics entirely and barks: "Got to/got to/got to/got to...." No wonder Janis Joplin attended every Otis Redding concert she could, standing close to the stage and, in essence, going to school on Otis so she could learn how he made his songs --- to use her word --- "visible."

One reason Redding was such an electrifying performer: He was like a track star who runs the mile --- but treats it like a sprint. As a result, everything about this ten song CD violates the conventions of live recording. If you start with a flat-out screamer like "Respect," nine out of ten singers will slow it down in the second song --- unless you're Otis Redding and you're in a mood to do "I Can't Turn You Loose" at a pace usually described as "pile-driving." He then comes to a full stop with a wrenching "I've Been Loving You Too Long (To Stop Now)." He picks it up again with Smokey Robinson's "My Girl" and Sam Cooke's "Shake." And follows that with a version of "Satisfaction" that makes Jagger and the Stones sound like slackers.

Two ballads follow, then a dash through the Beatles "Day Tripper," and before you know it, there's one song left.

It is "Try a Little Tenderness," and if you know it, you know it's about women who will never have pretty clothes and expensive trips and homes that are featured in magazines. That's no one's fault: They're married to men who, more often than not, make their living with their muscles and are often just a paycheck or two ahead of trouble. These men love their women --- but how can they prove it?

In the gospel according to Otis, there's only one way: show your love. "You've got to hold her/squeeze her/never leave her".... and from here, Otis leaves language behind, rushing headlong from "got to/got to" to sounds so primitive and immediate, sounds so intimate, you almost feel you shouldn't be listening.

Otis Redding began his career in high school. His family was poor; the school had a talent show with a $5 first prize. He won 15 straight times before the school refused to let him compete. At 18, he turned pro. By 20, it was clear he was soul's best singer.

"Otis Redding Live in Europe" was recorded in March of 1967 and released that June. On December 10th of that year, a plane carrying Redding and his band crashed into a Wisconsin lake. Four members of the band died. And so, alas, did Otis. He was 26.∎

MUSIC

WORLD

Amadou & Mariam

Do you like music that makes you happy? I don't mean moderately happy, 7.5 on a scale of 10, isn't it a great day happy, kind of sort of happy.

I mean ecstatic, get up and dance happy, throw caution to the winds and kiss a stranger happy, pump up the volume and wake your neighbors happy, see yourself realizing all your dreams happy.

Amadou Bagayoko and Mariam Doumbia are from Mali. They met in the 1970s, married in 1980 and started performing together. Like their fellow musicians from Mali --- I'm thinking of Ali Farka Toure and Boubacar Traore --- they started with their country's version of the blues. Along the way, they went international and borrowed from cultures as diverse as Cuba and France. And they became very popular indeed.

Small fact: They're blind. Both of them. And possessed of the unusual joy that is the special province of some of the unsighted.

In 2003, Amadou and Mariam hooked up with Manu Chao. This is major, for Chao is a world music god everywhere but in America. The reason for that is somewhat predictable: Chao is unabashedly political. Many of his lyrics are about poverty and oppression, his music is based on local folk music, and underneath it is usually a bouncy punk beat. (In 1994, he bought a train in Colombia, assembled a traveling circus and traveled the country, stopping in villages to perform. "People coming to the show, they all had a gun," he has recalled. "But we went through with no problem. That was our little victory.")

Chao not only produced "Dimanche a Bamako," he co-authored some of the songs, and sang and played guitar as well. But it's as a producer that he shines brightest. Almost every song has a killer beat, and on top of that he layers street sounds, harmonies from anywhere (this CD starts with a cross between 1960s hootenany and 1950s doo-wop), and on top of all that are Amadou and Mariam, who would be offended if they were ever described as less than "hypnotic."

"Dimanche à Bamako" was a huge hit in France, where it won a Les Victoires de la Musique award (the French Grammy). Just from "La Realite" --- the song I can hear over and over --- I can understand why. The music has police whistles, xylophone, sirens, cheering crowds, a Tex-Mex organ and a beat that pounds disco right through the wall into reggae's yard.

And the lyrics (in French) have a brilliantly calibrated mix of rebel politics, weary philosophy and, finally, a command to get out of the chair:

Ups and downs
It is life in this world
Sad reality
While some are being born
Others are dying
And while some are laughing others are crying
Ups and downs
It is life in this world
Sad reality

Some have work while others are out of work
Then it must be that while some are sleeping
Others are keeping the watch
It is the sad reality
But...let us dance together

Exciting? Thrilling! As the distinguished English critic Charlie Gillett has written, "There are going to be many people who will find they have three copies of this album by the end of this year: one that they bought themselves, the other two given by people who'll say, 'I heard this and thought this is the kind of thing you like.' And there will be people who will themselves have bought three or four copies to give to friends, saying, 'I know you've sworn you'll never like an album not in English, but this is the one to win you over.'"

I'll say it more bluntly: This is pure joy, suitable for every occasion. To turn away from "Dimanche a Bamako" is to choose to live a diminished life. I beg you: Don't miss this one. ■

BOMBINO

He had scorched the Newport Folk Festival --- "three kaftans soaked, the crowd went nuts," my correspondent reported --- and now it was time for Brooklyn. I lured others into a Head Butler Field Trip and off we went.

There was as much to look at as there was to hear. Bombino was flanked by two guitarists, swathed in white like the Magi. The effect is spooky; you're very aware of the distance this man, his band and his music have traveled and how great is the gulf between our cultures.

And, yes, it's strange music. The foundation is a drummer who plays tight, clipped, ruthlessly propulsive time. And then it's all guitars: thundering, amped-up bass and rhythm. And then Bombino, amazingly inventive, constantly surprising, musical to the core. And dancing --- not like any dance you've ever seen, more like a strut-and-stutter camel walk.

His most recent CD, "Nomad," is 40 minutes of protein-rich music: great for parties (you will come to be bored by friends asking "What is that?"), a lifesaver on rainy mornings when you don't want to get out of bed, a good candidate for serious listening, a caffeine hit for long sessions of work when your friends are getting buzzed on Adderall, and, so far from least, an essential ingredient for ecstatic couplings at midnight.

What's so great? First the writing: it's all hooks. Hooks upon hooks until you are locked in a groove. But it's mostly Omara "Bombino" Moctar's guitar. It slithers. It buzzes. It's round like Knopfler, spacy like Hendrix, concise like Ali Farka Toure. And he has a great producer: Dan Auerbach, who is half of The Black Keys, a band that proves again and again that when you're mega-talented, a guitarist and a drummer are all you need.

The back story: Omara Moctar was born in 1980. He's a Tuareg. (Volkswagen named its off-road SUV after this tribe of desert nomads in Niger.) The Tuareg, who are descended from the Berbers of North Africa, are fiercely independent. Once they fought against colonialism. Now, although they're Muslims, they resist Islamic fundamentalism. ("These invaders from Mali are not welcome in any of our lands," Moctar says. "We reject their philosophies and their idea of Islam.")

In the 1990s, civil war wracked Niger. The Tuaregs were declared enemies of the state. Moctar and his family fled to Algeria. Relatives brought guitars, and Moctar learned to play. Fighting subsided. Moctar's family returned to Niger. But in 2007, when he'd launched a band, there was a second Taureg rebellion and a harsher government response. Two of Moctar's musicians were killed; Moctar fled to Burkina Faso.

On his first, under-the-radar America tour, Moctar met Dan Auerbach. They had no common language, but a short session of music made it clear they could collaborate. Auerbach: "He would triple his guitar leads, and he'd do it note-for-note, first take. It sounds massive. His guitar's running through fuzz pedals, with double drummers playing at the same time -- lots of percussion."

Translation: This is desert music, but it's been processed in a Nashville studio. Not to trick it up, but to make it stronger. And it is. There are no English lyrics; because they're in a language you don't speak, the words have power only as sounds. They suffice.■

Cesaria Evora

Sao Vicente is one of the Cape Verde islands, 350 miles off the coast of Senegal. These ten small islands are so wind-blasted and desolate that they were uninhabited until 1462. Four centuries of exploitation followed.

It was Cesaria Evora's fate to be born there. Geography was destiny for her --- her voice was the living soul of Cape Verde. Given its history and culture, you really couldn't expect the islands' muse to fill her CDs with songs that make you want to dance.

In fact, Cesaria Evora's specialty was morna, an intensely melancholy, minor-key music, sung mostly in Portuguese. But for Evora, Cape Verde's musical tradition was only the first reason that her songs were odes to longing and regret. Although she was a local star by 20, she never left the islands until she was in her mid-forties, when she finally made her first recordings.

It wasn't until her 50s that she became the darling of the world-music crowd. She still performed shoeless, to express her solidarity with her impoverished countrymen. She still stopped singing in mid-concert to sit at a small table and smoke a cigarette. And she never veered from the music she'd made for decades; the last thing on her mind, it seemed, was mass success.

I interviewed her when she was 60. Her English wasn't strong, so she brought along a translator. After a while, we switched to French --- easier for her, harder for me. But her irony and wit came through quite clearly.

JK: When you're onstage and you take that cigarette break, you seem a million miles away. Are you?

CE: No. I'm taking a break because I'm addicted to cigarettes. So I relax and enjoy it.

JK: In a rare upbeat song, you sing, "God gave us the world to live happily in." Do you live happily?

CE: I'm not a sad person. But in life, there are so many moments when you have to be sad. It's all in the moment.

JK: I read that you've been left by three husbands. And then you said, "No man shall ever sleep again under my roof." True?

CE: I've never married. I've had three kids with different men. And I still like men. And what I'm sure I said was "I don't have a husband with me all the time."

JK: You stopped singing for ten years. How painful was that?

CE: Not. I was working and not getting any results, so I decided to stop. In '85, I got some work, so I started again.

JK: What is a day like for you in Cape Verde?

CE: I have a completely normal life. I take care of my house, I visit with family and friends. At night I sometimes go out. Whatever the rest of the world may think of me now, I was always considered a great singer at home. But we all know each other. There's no "stardom" in Cape Verde.

The last time I saw Evora in concert, she came onstage in a simple dress and delivered two dozen exquisitely mournful songs. Then, for the final encore, the band played with an energy and rhythm that was first cousin to the Cuban jazz of the Buena Vista Social Club.

The crowd was on its feet, hands over heads, clapping and dancing. The only person in the theater who seemed unmoved was Evora, who stood apart, stolidly accepting their love.

At last, she spoke just two words: "Obligado. Terminée." And then she permitted herself one small, delicious shimmy. ∎

Nusrat Fateh Ali Khan

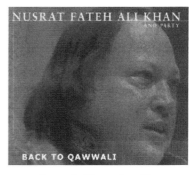

NUSRAT FATEH ALI KHAN
AND PARTY

BACK TO QAWWALI

What singer was bigger than Elvis?
Nusrat Fateh Ali Khan.

But unless you haunt the "World Music" bins, the name is probably unfamiliar. That's not the case anywhere else in the world; music lovers in Europe, Asia and the Middle East are well aware that Nusrat recorded some 125 CDs. And that he was very possibly the greatest blues singer on the planet --- I read somewhere that Van Morrison called Nusrat the greatest singer, period.

Blues singer?

I take only slight liberties here. In fact, Nusrat was a Pakistani Qawaali singer. His family had been singers for six hundred years; at 16, his father died and he was drafted into his family's singing group. Perfect timing: Qawaali was about to change from music inspired by Sufi prayers to music that merged spirituality with technology.

Traditional Qawwaali has a fairly strict form, as devotional music often does: a lead singer and a backup group called a "party." Groups tend to have nine musicians --- five singers, a harmonium player, some drummers. A typical song lasts 15 minutes or so, but not because there are hundreds of stanzas; singers quickly move away from lyrics filled with praise for God to the kind of call-and-response that Americans tend to associate with Baptist church music in the black neighborhoods of the South.

Nusrat began with improvisation --- and then took a sudden leap into a sustained, ecstatic solo. The late Jeff Buckley described his first experience of hearing the voice of Nusrat, and nailed what it was like to be knocked back by his power:

I was all-awash in the thick undulating tide of dark Punjabi tabla rhythms, spiked with synchronized handclaps booming from above and below in hard, perfect time. I heard the clarion call of harmoniums dancing the antique melody around like giant, singing wooden spiders. Then, all of a sudden, the rising of one, then ten voices hovering over the tone like a flock of geese ascending into formation across the sky. Then came the voice of Nusrat Fateh Ali Khan. His voice is velvet-fire, simply incomparable. I knew not one word of Urdu, and somehow it still hooked me into a story that he wove with his wordless voice. Melody after melody crashed upon each other in waves of improvisations; with each line being repeated by the men in chorus, restated again by the main soloists, and then Nusrat setting the whole bloody thing aflame with his rapid-fire scatting. The phrase burst into a climax somewhere, with Nusrat's upper register painting a melody that made my heart long to fly. The piece went on for fifteen minutes. I ate my heart out. I felt a rush of adrenaline in my chest, like I was on the edge of a cliff, wondering when I would jump and how will the ocean catch me.

Jeff Buckley was a late convert. Along the way Nusrat was taken up by Imran Khan, the captain of the Pakistani cricket team and a national hero. That led to soundtracks for Indian films. That brought his work to the attention of Eddie Vedder and Peter Gabriel, who used his music in "Dead Man Walking" and "The Last Temptation of Christ."

With those films, Nusrat was poised for American success. Alas, Nusrat was a large man, and a diabetic. In 1997, he was on his way to London for treatment when he died. He was just 49.

Nusrat is important not only for his glorious musical achievement, but as a champion of tolerance and understanding. Muslims, Hindus and Sufis all found inspiration in his music; his concerts were love fests. In the CDs, you can also feel the love. ■

Bob Marley & The Wailers

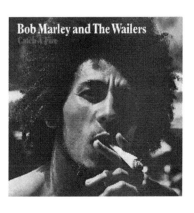
Bob Marley and The Wailers

Think back to 1973. The great rock revolution of the '60s was over. Music had become what it is now: a business. A depressing time.

And then, at Max's Kansas City, I found what I had been seeking. Some friends of friends were playing; an unknown group called The Wailers was on the bill. These young Jamaicans came out, freaky as Sly Stone, clearly tranced-out behind some serious ganja, and began to play amazingly complicated music that had me twisting in one direction while the beat had me going in another.

Excited and limp, I went backstage (back then, back there, no big deal). Met the Wailers (Bob Marley was not then The Star). And, the next day, bought "Catch A Fire," their American debut.

There are two versions of the album cover. One is a rendition of a Zippo lighter (it opens — and, very quickly, breaks). The other features Marley smoking a huge spliff. That one came later. I got the original.

And was it ever original. There were sweet seduction songs. There were songs that evoked Jamaica's colonial past. Angry political songs: "No chains around my feet/ But I'm not free/I know I am bound here in captivity..." And the spooky Rasta dreamscape, "Midnight Ravers," with its devastating opening condemnation ("You can't tell the women from the men/ 'cause they're dressed in the same pollution") and its Book of Revelations vision ("I see ten thousand chariots/And they coming without horses/The riders — they cover their faces/So you couldn't make them out in smoky place").

Rarely has music been better matched to lyrics. "Midnight Ravers" is the best example. A repeated corskscrew organ riff. Guitars that sting, then soar. And a bass guitar/drum pattern that paints a musical picture of camel-like horses riding, riding, riding, in the dead of night.

One night, in a Philadelphia club, I had dinner with The Wailers in their dressing room and watched them smoke so much ganja they should have passed out.

Instead, they went on stage and — like angels, or aliens, or just humans blessed with telepathy — played a note-perfect set that converted everyone in the room to blithering fandom.

The sanctification of Bob Marley began the following year. There was only one more true Wailers album ("Burnin'") before the band changed. And then came all the songs you know — great songs, but great in isolation, like great singles. "Catch A Fire," on the other hand, is a great album: there's a logic to the flow of the songs, a satisfaction that's bigger than the sum of the individual tunes.

One afternoon, I went down to the Chelsea Hotel to suggest a movie to Marley. Before I could tell him my ideas, he put his spliff down long enough to draw a square on a piece of paper. "This one is us," he said. He drew another square. "This one is the bank." He drew a connecting line, looked up at me and grinned — and our movie died right there.

You may own the greatest hits. But do you have the greatest album? Not until you have this. ■

HOLIDAY

Phil Spector:
A Christmas Gift for You

Phil Spector is a killer and a sleaze, but he is also a tragedy.

When he was ten years old, his father connected a hose to the exhaust pipe of the family car.

Later, his mother chased him around the kitchen, brandishing a knife and shouting, "Your father killed himself because you were a bad child."

He was small and asthmatic, bullied in school.

And, at 20, he had his first #1 hit: "To Know Him Is To Love Him", a title borrowed from the epitaph on his father's grave.

The hits kept on coming; as a writer and producer, he was magic, both with black groups (The Ronettes, Crystals, Ben E. King and more) and white (The Righteous Brothers).

In 1967, he released his masterpiece, "River Deep Mountain High." Tina Turner sang her guts out, but everyone on that massive production was simply company for Spector. This was his Wagnerian opera, this was the "wall of sound" as it had never been heard before. Artistically, it's thrilling. Commercially, it flopped. And after that, Spector was troubled, haunted and dangerous.

The creator who had been obsessed with making "little symphonies for the kids" now turned his attention to situations he could control. He allegedly locked his wife, Ronnie Spector, in a closet to teach her a lesson. Another time, he had a gold coffin constructed with a glass top and threatened her: "If you leave me, I'll kill you and put you on display." He held a gun to Leonard Cohen's head and said, "I love you, Leonard" — to which Cohen responded, "I hope you do, Phil." Add a mountain of cocaine and increasing isolation, and ruin was just a matter of time and place.

There are many morals to the Phil Spector story for those who like to see morals in biographies, but I prefer to turn away from this sad tale to what may well have been Spector's greatest triumph.

I mean: "A Christmas Gift for You," his 1963 holiday album, released on the day John K. Kennedy was assassinated. Unsurprisingly, it was a flop. But it's the best holiday album ever made.

And that's not just my view. Read through the reviews, check the books and rock bards. Everyone says the same thing: the.... best... holiday... record... ever... made. ■

THE SNOWMAN

The best holiday stories are fables. "Believe," they instruct us. "Love," they dare us. "Trust," they implore us.

And the child in us — connecting with the child who inspired the holiday — responds. "Yes," we say, eyes misting, because we so want it to be true. And because, looking down at our kids, we feel we know that it is true.

Sometimes the fables work right through the holidays. Sometimes they inspire us whenever we dip into them.

"The Snowman" has that power.

The 23-minute animated film directed by Dianne Jackson was adapted in 1982 from the 32-page book by Raymond Briggs.

Don't know Briggs? There's a reason. He's English. He works as a freelance illustrator, book designer and writer of what are known as "children's books." They're anything but. Oh, kids adore them --- when our daughter was 3, she could watch "The Snowman" half a dozen times --- but they function quite well, or maybe even better, as books for adults.

The first reason for the appeal of "The Snowman" is its deceptively simple story. A boy in rural England builds a snowman. At midnight, as the boy looks out his window, the snowman lights up. The boy runs outside. He invites the snowman to tour his home. Then the snowman takes his hand. And off they fly, over England, over water, to the North Pole.

Santa gives the boy a scarf. The boy and the snowman fly home. As the boy is going inside, the snowman waves --- a wave of goodbye. The boy rushes into his arms and hugs him. The next morning, the snowman's just a few lumps of coal and an old hat.

Did that magical night really happen? The boy reaches into his pocket and finds the scarf. He drops to his knees and, almost as an offering, places it by the snowman's hat.

A desolate ending? Yes and no. Yes, if you get stuck on the facts: the boy's alone again. No, if you are taken by the boy's magical experience with a special, secret friend --- he's been given a night of exquisite sweetness that will forever be his to cherish. That's not too deep for kids; they'll be more fixated on the magic than its loss.

Then there is the artistry. This is not machine-driven animation --- Briggs works with colored pencil. "I once kept a record of the time it took to do two pages," he told an interviewer. "Penciling: 20 hours. Inking: 18 hours. Coloring: 25 hours. And all that's after months of getting ideas, writing and planning."

And the feelings in "The Snowman" couldn't be more personal. The boy's house? That is Briggs's own house and garden in Sussex. The flight over the South Downs and the top of Brighton 's Royal Pavilion to Brighton Pier --- those are old Briggs haunts.

The final appeal is to beauty. The film begins with Briggs walking across a field, talking about the snowstorm. From then on, the film is silent, except for a song. It is called "Walking In The Air," and it is life-changing --- the sequence when the boy and the snowman start to fly and the song comes in is one of the greatest moments in film. Period.

I once had a job helping several hundred people be better writers. There were two hobby-horses I rode continually: "Whenever you use the word 'hopefully,' you are using it incorrectly. And there is no such thing as 'perfect.'" I was wrong. There is perfect. "The Snowman" defines it. ∎

Chris Van Allsburg: The Polar Express

What is the most interactive medium of all?

A rich, wise man in Silicon Valley --- so rich he did not need to offer up the kneejerk response: "online media" --- had the right answer:

A person in a chair, reading a book.

I instinctively knew that was right. As, surely, do you. For we have all had that magic experience of opening a book and entering a drama of knights and knaves, princes and goddesses. This world? We've left it. We are living the book.

But I would go one step further: The most interactive medium of all is a person in a chair, *reading a book to a child.*

Especially this book.

On Christmas Eve, a father tells his son that there's no Santa Claus. Later that night, a train packed with children stops in front of a boy's house. He hops on and travels to the North Pole, where Santa offers him the first toy of Christmas. The boy chooses a reindeer's bell. On the way home, he loses it. How he finds it and what that means --- that's where you reach for the Kleenex.

A simple story. A timeless story, and on purpose --- as Van Allsburg has said, "If you opened up my books and there was no copyright page, you wouldn't be able to tell exactly when it was published." It's precisely because the illustrations do not anchor us to our time, our town, that we can deal more directly with the theme of the book.

That theme is belief. Not in Santa, though that will do just fine for kids. Belief in really big things, things we hope are true even in the face of all the information that says they are not. Again, Van Allsburg: "We can believe that extraordinary things can happen. We can believe fantastic things that might happen. Or we can believe that what we see is what we get. But if all that I believe in is what I can see, then the world is a smaller, less interesting place."

Sometimes I believe in magic. Sometimes I believe in miracles. That is the baseline of all the greatest spiritual stories --- the impossible happens. And you can't explain it. Except, perhaps, as C.S. Lewis does: "Miracles only occur to people who believe in them."

So as your holiday gift to yourself, buy the book. Not the "special edition" with the bell and the CD and Lord knows what else. Not the Kindle download. The basic book. Because it's all you need.

And then, of course, find a child. And settle in your chair. And start to read. Before you know it, your eyes will mist, you'll be reaching for the Kleenex, and --- and this is the best part of all, especially for the sophisticated and the hard of heart and the bitterly disappointed --- you will believe. ■

MOVIES

"A Face in the Crowd"

Lonesome Rhodes, media rocket, got his start in jail. When we first see him, he's a drifter doing short time in Arkansas. He's cheerful, handsome, and, in a good ole boy way, mildly charismatic --- he's Andy Griffith, in his first movie role.

Marcia Jeffries (Patricia Neal) shows up. She's got a radio show called "A Face in the Crowd." Its premise: Everyone has talent. And here's Larry Rhodes, strumming his old "Mama Git-tar." Of course this Sarah Lawrence graduate is going to switch on her tape recorder while he sings an original song called "Free Man in the Morning."

Romance follows. So does an audience. Soon he's got a national TV show and big time sponsors. Ah, TV. It's just made for a guy like Lonesome.

This is not the Andy Griffith we'll come to love in "Mayberry R.F.D." He's a drifter not because he's had some bad luck but because he's a blowhard, an egomaniac and a fraud. And the train he's riding always has the same destination: a crude populism that's really all about him.

Maybe the suckers can't grasp his contempt for them, but they do grasp who's always seen with Lonesome: a woman. They're everywhere for him. So Lonesome passes over Marcia to marry a high school cheerleader (Lee Remick, in her film debut). No bets on how long he'll be faithful to her....

This 1957 film was written by Budd Schulberg and directed by Elia Kazan --- the team that created "On the Waterfront." That 1954 film won eight Academy Awards, including Best Picture, Best Actor and Best Director. This film? A classic --- but it won no Oscars.

It wasn't just that Americans knew the film was loosely based on Arthur Godfrey, a lovable television host with a big dark side. I suspect it was also the subject matter: the conning of the mass audience. Because the thing is, people --- and Americans in particular --- love being conned. Given the choice between a simple lie and a complex, ambiguous truth, we vote for the lie. And we don't thank you if you puncture our balloon.

"A Face in the Crowd" punctures many balloons. ∎

"AFTER THE WEDDING"

This could be the best film I've seen in a decade.

And I say that even though I didn't see all of it --- like just about everyone else in that theater, for the entire last half hour I was afflicted by a bout of silent sobbing that wouldn't quit.

I cherish that amazing, unforgettable experience: several hundred people weeping together. And then --- I'm not spoiling the movie here --- came a "happy ending" that is perhaps the most satisfying conclusion of any film I've seen in a decade.

Satisfying because the characters earned it. There was a huge price for each of them to pay, and they stepped up to it. They earned the right to better. And, because you have lived their struggles with them, you leave the movie with the kind of satisfaction that no studio-financed, movie-by-committee-and-focus-group can give you.

The story is pure soap opera. Really. On a low budget, with no-name actors and maybe even this script, "After the Wedding" would be right at home on Lifetime. Consider the plot. Jacob, a Dane in his 30s, works in an orphanage in India. He hasn't been home in 20 years, and that's just fine with him. Bad news: The orphanage is running out of money. Good news: Jørgen, a philanthropist, wants to write the large check that will save it. On one condition: He wants to meet the recipient. The woman who runs the orphanage can't go. Well, Jørgen is Danish, Jacob is Danish. Jacob should go.

Reluctantly, Jacob flies to Denmark. Jørgen listens to his pitch for only a few minutes before seeming to lose interest --- it's the weekend of his daughter's wedding. To which Jacob should come. It's not, after all, like he has anything else to do.

At the wedding, the first surprise: Helene, Jørgen's wife, was once Jacob's lover. In fact, she was the lover who broke his heart. The lover who sent him scurrying off to India, an orphan hiding among orphans.

Other surprises: I'll spare you. And encourage you to read not a word more about the story --- let the twists and turns sear you as they roll out. But I'll go this far: The rich and poor, the white and the colored, Europeans and Indians --- the moral lessons are so easy, aren't they? Or are they? Is Jacob's moral purity really an emblem of superiority? Is Jørgen's privileged life a sign of a rotting soul? You'll judge --- you can't help it --- but when it's over... when it's over, you'll want to thank director Susanne Bier.

"After the Wedding" was Denmark's entry for Best Foreign Language Film at the 2007 Academy Awards. It lost to the German film, "The Lives of Others." I might have voted differently. ∎

"Battle of Algiers"

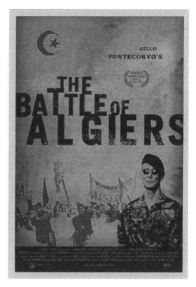

Almost every war movie stacks the deck. Enemy soldiers wear dark clothes, are unshaven, speak in accents and die in large numbers at the end. Heroes are played by actors who get $10 to $20 million a film; of course they get to go home and pick up their lives where they left off.

Moral complexity? Not that you can notice --- war movies are like Westerns, just with better weapons.

Political movies are no better. The filmmaker --- if not the studio --- is on one "side" or other. The movie is a function of its point-of-view.

What if there were a political film without a hero? A war movie that doesn't take sides?

"Battle of Algiers" is that film. It is not only one of the greatest movies about conflict, it is, according to many critics and this unabashed fan, one of the greatest films ever made --- so great that no one has been able to steal from it.

"Battle of Algiers" is rooted in fact. It covers the period from 1954 to 1957, when Algeria was a colony of France and Algeria's National Liberation Front led uprisings in Algiers. French troops were sent in. The revolt was crushed.

But the movie is not the record of a victory or a defeat. It's about what makes people cry "Enough" and do something about it. It's about the cost of conflict and the loss of innocent life. And it's about the tide of history --- in this case, about what may be the inevitable result of colonial occupation.

The movie looks like a documentary, shot in black-and-white --- but there is not one frame of historical footage in the film. As for actors, there are 150 amateurs in the film. The only professional is the French Colonel. The Algerian boy who plays Ali La Pointe was an illiterate street kid with no acting experience. Journalists and French soldiers were played by tourists.

Pontecorvo doesn't take sides. He doesn't even have a designated hero.

He's following a "collective protagonist" on the Algerian side and the power of France --- personified by Colonel Mathieu, who was a Resistance fighter during World War II --- on the other.

"Battle of Algiers" is one of the most controversial films ever made. When it was re-leased in 1967, it was widely honored --- it won the Grand Prize at the Venice Film Festival and was nominated for three Academy Awards, including Best Screenplay (Gillo Pontecorvo and Franco Solinas), Best Director and Best Foreign Language Film.

But it was banned in France until 1971 after some theaters showing it were bombed. For a decade or so, it was used in the Middle East as a training film for insurgents --- with noisy projectors and sheets for screens. And in 2003, the Directorate for Special Operations and Low-Intensity Conflict at the Pentagon screened the film as a possible scenario of what American troops might face in Iraq.

The plot: Ali La Pointe is a petty criminal in jail for a minor offense. There he sees an execution of a fellow Algerian whose last words are "Allah is great! Long live Al-geria!" When he's released, Ali is recruited by the National Liberation Front, which has developed an effective new tactic --- making war on French civilians.

This splits the viewer down the middle. It's very hard to cheer the French, but what can you say about people who put bombs in coffee shops and blow up high school kids? Does the end justify the means? If not, how do you effectively break the yoke of colonial oppression?

For all the action scenes --- and "Battle of Algiers" has some of the most astonishing street fights and scenes of "terrorism" ever filmed --- it's the conflict of ideas that's most stinging. Here's a news conference with a captured freedom fighter:

Journalist: M. Ben M'Hidi, don't you think it's a bit cowardly to use women's baskets and handbags to carry explosive devices that kill so many innocent people?

Ben M'Hidi: And doesn't it seem to you even more cowardly to drop napalm bombs on defenseless villages, so that there are a thousand times more innocent victims? Of course, if we had your airplanes it would be a lot easier for us. Give us your bombers, and you can have our baskets.

Most of all, there is a compelling argument about the wisdom and effectiveness of torture. Here's the leader of the French Army in Algiers:

Col. Mathieu: The word "torture" doesn't appear in our orders. We've always spoken of interrogation as the only valid method in a police operation directed against unknown enemies. As for the NLF, they request that their members, in the event of capture, should maintain silence for twenty-four hours, and then they may talk. So the organization has already had the time it needs to render any information useless. What type of interroga-

tion should we choose, the one the courts use for a murder case, that drags on for months? ... Should we remain in Algeria? If you answer "yes," then you must accept all the necessary consequences.

The music --- by Ennio Morricone, who scored Sergio Leone's "spaghetti westerns" --- will haunt and agitate you. And when you see what happens at the end of the film, you'll know why I tell you that your heart level will definitely elevate.

The film is in French. The subtitles are large and clear. But you don't need to hear the sound to understand the plot. Understanding the message is much more difficult. Indeed, forty years after "Battle of Algiers" was released, its issues are the biggest international challenge we face.

If you love movies, this is necessary viewing. ∎

"Dodsworth"

Here's a checklist of elements you'd never see in a movie financed by an American studio today:

-- a middle-aged love story.
-- with infidelity on the part of the wife.
-- Oh, and she isn't a despicable slut.
-- Oh, and her husband keeps trying to make the marriage work.

"Dodsworth" is adapted from a novel by the underrated Sinclair Lewis. It's a terrific book: vivid, fast-paced, deeply satisfying. Lewis and playwright Sidney Howard (who'd go on to win an Academy Award for his adaptation of "Gone with the Wind") collaborated on the screenplay.

The other collaboration --- their first --- was between producer Sam Goldwyn and director William Wyler, perhaps the greatest Hollywood director of the 1930s and 1940s, and certainly the most underrated. (Wyler directed "Ben-Hur," "The Best Years of Our Lives," "Mrs. Miniver," "Roman Holiday," "The Letter," "Wuthering Heights" and "Funny Girl" --- get the idea?)

The story is a simple one: Samuel Dodsworth (Walter Huston) is a rich Midwestern industrialist who sells his business and sets out to "enjoy life." His wife Fran (Ruth Chatterton) couldn't agree more --- her daughter is just married, and the thought of growing old appalls her. She wants to be chic, she wants "to live." She is, in short, a bomb waiting to explode.

Off the Dodsworths sail to Europe. They have barely waved goodbye to New York when Fran encounters her first suitor. She leads him on, then is shocked when he makes advances --- she's really not very good at this game. And she doesn't get better; she has a knack for falling "in love" with any Count of No Account who crosses her path.

Paul Lukas, David Niven, Gregory Gaye --- Fran's suitors come and go, as Sam tolerates her escalating insults. But Sam is no wimp. When he snaps, he is firm and manly and smart all at once.

There's a confrontation scene in a Paris hotel room. Sam. Fran. A lover. The oldest, saddest triangle. It could have been shot to reflect the tension. Instead, Wyler's camera circles the threesome. It's dazzling filmmaking.

But then, every element of the film dazzles. Especially the acting. These are complicated, sophisticated roles --- the characters aren't cardboard saints and demons, but conflicted, well-meaning people who remind us of ourselves (or, at least, People We Know). Every actor, even the young and callow, suggests a complexity we rarely see in movies today. And Sam Dodsworth's speech at the breaking point --- "Love has to stop short of suicide" --- strikes just the right note of determination and poignancy.

"Dodsworth" was nominated for seven Academy Awards in 1937, including Best Picture, Best Director and Best Writing, Screenplay. It only won for Art Direction. Robbery, I tell you. Robbery. ■

"L'Atalante"

The movie was made in winter. And on the river. Jean Vigo was already suffering from tuberculosis. Now he got so sick he sometimes had to direct from a cot. His illness worsened when he finished the film, and, again, when it was released. For the studio had hated the movie, re-cut it, added a popular song to the soundtrack, changed the title and slammed it into theaters --- as an entertainment "inspired by" the song.

Thirty-four days after he handed "L'Atalante" over to the studio, Jean Vigo died. His distraught wife tried to join him in death by jumping out a window. Luckily, friends grabbed her in mid-stride. But she had it right: Jean Vigo's death in 1934 was a tragedy. He had directed only a few films. He had just made a great movie. More were surely ordained. But there it was. Death. At 29.

The film in question is now on almost every critic's list of the "best 100 movies of all time." And not near the bottom --- I've never seen it ranked lower than #15. After Renoir's "Rules of the Game," it's the highest ranked French film. But although it was brilliantly restored in 1990, few Americans know about "L'Atalante." Fewer have seen it.

The story is so simple you may wonder how Vigo filled 87 minutes with it. Jean is the young captain of L'Atalante, a barge that goes up and down the Seine. He marries Juliette, a country girl who has never left her village. Now she's on a boat making its slow way to Paris. And she's the only woman --- the crew is a colorful old salt named Pere Jules and his son.

For someone as provincial as Juliette, married life and barge life are a double shock. When the barge reaches Paris, Jean and Juliette quarrel. She runs off. He can't find her. They miss each other horribly. They're reunited. End of movie.

Vigo inherited what looks like a banal story from the studio. He hired Boris Kaufman --- who would later come to America and shoot "On the Waterfront" --- as the cinematographer. And then he added the touches that make this film so extraordinary: the tenderness of the relationship set against the rough, documentary feel of life on the barge, the silvery beauty of the boat moving through fog, the almost surrealistic shots of Juliette in her wedding gown on the deck of the barge, the mesmerizing underwater sequence.

Truffaut said that, by filming ordinary people doing ordinary things, Vigo achieved poetry. I'd go further --- he finds the poetry in ordinary people. The night Jean and Juliette are separated, for example. Vigo cuts back and forth, showing their loneliness --- and, in a daring sequence, showing them caress themselves. It's a powerful erotic moment. But its power comes from its universality, its commonness.

Why is "L'Atalante" so highly regarded? To see it is to know. ■

"McCabe & Mrs. Miller"

Robert Altman liked to say he hated Westerns. He didn't much enjoy working with Warren Beatty. He was silent about directing Julie Christie. He probably disliked her too.

But in the winter of 1970, Altman took Beatty and Christie to the Pacific Northwest and made one of the best Westerns I've ever seen.

Well, not exactly a Western as you may think of it.

In 1970, our President was a crook, we were locked in an Asian war we could not win, our kids were growing their hair long, smoking weed and fornicating in the stairwells.

With that going on, no way does Robert Altman make a traditional Western.

This movie is about much more than the plot, but here's the plot: Warren Beatty (McCabe), a small-time gambler with more dreams than brains, comes to the tiny community of Presbyterian Church to open a bar and bordello. It is his great good fortune to run into Julie Christie (Mrs. Miller), an opium-smoking prostitute who actually knows how to run a whorehouse. They join forces, get successful, start an awkward romance.

A corporation decides to buy them out. Christie's in favor of the deal --- she understands the power of Big Business --- but Beattie fancies himself a negotiator. So the corporation dispatches three gunmen to kill him.

I was just out of college when "McCabe & Mrs. Miller" was released. I was a disciple of Leonard Cohen (whose early songs provide a gloomy, dreamy soundtrack). I admired Altman, respected Beatty, had a crush on Christie. My reaction to the film was predictable: It was one of the greater films I'd ever seen.

Most critics didn't agree. Here's Vincent Canby, of The New York Times: "The intentions of 'McCabe & Mrs. Miller' are... meddlesomely imposed on the film by tired symbolism, by a folk-song commentary on the soundtrack... and by metaphysically purposeful photography... Such intentions keep spoiling the fun of what might have been an uproarious frontier fable."

Talk about wrong-headed! Canby wanted Altman to make another "M*A*S*H." Altman had no interest in that. He wanted to get inside a genre, to show that the West wasn't Gary Cooper and John Wayne --- it was just like now, with little people starting small enterprises and getting a town going, then the Big Boys muscling them out and sucking the soul from the community. The story of the hardware store and Wal-Mart. Kind of the domestic story of our time....

But "McCabe & Mrs. Miller" is no more about its plot than your life is. It's about dreams. And wanting to build something for yourself when you're over your head and you don't really know the players and all you have is you. And then it's about taking the next step --- gambling on love, on dreams. The Leonard Cohen lyric about the gambler says it all: "He's just looking for a card so high and wild he'll never have to deal another."

And then it's about weather. First drizzle, then snow. And as the snow blankets the town, the movie gets quieter and quieter. The climax is inevitable and dark; it's played out in bright, silent snow. What ends badly also ends beautifully --- so beautifully that you can only imagine what lies Altman told to get the money for this film. ∎

"My Neighbor Totoro"

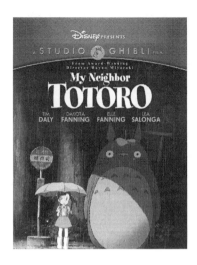

Every afternoon, when I'd meet our then eight-year-old at the camp bus, I'd ask about her day.

Perfunctory answers escaped her ecosystem. But not much more. This is, after all, a girl who used to tell us her favorite sport is "getting into bed."

So it was quite the surprise to see our daughter rush off the camp bus, mouth engaged, face flushed. They'd had a film at camp. The best she'd ever seen. Couldn't wait to see it again.

It was "My Neighbor Totoro," a 1988 animated feature written and directed by Hayao Miyazaki, who's best known for "Princess Mononoke," the 1997 film that was the first animated feature to win Japan's Best Picture of the Year. He then made "Spirited Away," which was even more successful. And then he made "Ponyo."

Here's the crazy thing. Our daughter had seen all of Miyazaki's later movies. They left her cold. Only "My Neighbor Totoro" gripped her and wouldn't let go.

I've watched "My Neighbor Totoro" again with the kid. I might come to disagree with her on Miyazaki's other films --- I've seen none of them --- but she is absolutely correct in her five-star assessment of "Totoro." No matter how old you are, no matter how sophisticated you may think you are, it is a fantastic film experience, an 86-minute swath of gorgeousness with a message as beautiful as its images.

And the trick of it is... there's no trick.

This is a movie rooted in the very ordinary.

When the film begins, it's 1958. Satsuki and Mei Kusakabe, eight and four years old, are driving with their father to their new home in the country. Dad's a professor in the city, but their mother has tuberculosis and is recovering in a rural hospital, and they want to be near her.

In a Disney movie, the first few scenes of the film would dazzle. Not here. The girls help their dad move in. They explore their new house and the fields and forest around it. They are, in a word, grounded.

This grounding is deceptive. Magic is afoot --- spirits only the young can see. Some are dust sprites, little balls of soot that dart around the rooms. (When they leave the house, racing toward the clouds on a moonlit night, your jaw might drop at the beauty.) And then there is Totoro, a large troll who lives in a giant tree. He bellows. He grins. But for the girls, he's really a big, soft climbing wall.

Stop the action for a moment, and look at what we have. Two leading characters, both girls. A loving father who, despite his work at a university, accepts the existence of spirits. A strange house that turns out to be warm and welcoming. A monster that isn't dangerous. In short, a world of harmony and understanding. The biggest problem here: When will Mom be healthy enough to come home for the weekend?

The sense of relief generated by all this wellbeing isn't boring. It's liberating. It allows us to explore with the girls, to laugh at the socially inept boy who lives nearby, and to wallow in the girls' adventures with the totoro.

The absence of conflict allows us to do something else: respond to the film's extravagant beauty. Miyazaki's a wonderful painter; if there was ever a film that makes you want to move to the country, this is it. The sky, the clouds, the forest --- this animation delivers more visual interest per frame than real-world photography. The totoro's genial awkwardness makes him fun to watch. And there's a Cat Bus that's just irresistible.

Late in the film, something may be going seriously wrong. The girls respond. So does dad. So do the totoro and the Cat Bus and the neighbors. What a smart little critic we have at home. What a wonderful world she introduced us to. ∎

"State of Play"

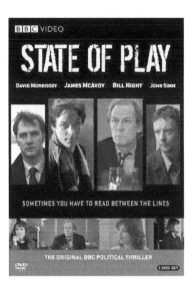

The editor in "State of Play" --- I mean the original version, not the dumbed-down flop of a remake starring Russell Crowe --- is determined, principled and witty, just what you expect from a Brit editor. He knows that Little People do the dirty work while the Mr. Bigs maintain their innocence. And he knows there's money, Murdoch-level money, that hums just below the surface, coloring every transaction.

Is a six-part BBC mini-series worth $28 on Amazon? Do the math --- it costs less than $5 an hour. A bargain. And ask yourself: When was the last time you watched six hours of anything and found yourself moving closer to the edge of your seat as it moved toward its conclusion?

That is the experience you'll have if you start watching "State of Play," a BBC mini-series that was broadcast in England in 2003 and later, to an assuredly smaller audience in the United States, on BBC's American channel. Now's it's a cult favorite on DVD.

"State of Play" starts simply. Sonia Baker falls to her death in the London subway --- ooops, tube --- station. Did she fall? Commit suicide? Or was she... pushed?

That's the last simple question in the mini-series. For, that same day, a kid gets killed in another part of London. No connection. Not possible, really --- Sonia Baker was a young research assistant to Steven Collins, chairman of the prestigious Energy Select Committee. The kid? A nobody.

At the newspaper, investigative reporter Cal McCaffrey and his colleagues start to dig. It just happens that Cal was once the campaign manager for Steven Collins. And has long had a crush on Collins' wife. A meaningless detail? Not when Cal learns that his old friend was having an affair with the research assistant --- and that Collins might have been planning to leave his wife for her.

From here, the complications multiply exponentially. For into the mix come politics, international oil companies and the corporate concerns of the paper's owners, to say nothing of their personal and professional conflicts. Add the romantic triangle, and the stew pot overflows. Smarties will love trying to stay current and think ahead.

Paul Abbott is a great screenwriter; there's not a flat character in the series. Cal seems troubled and underwhelming at the start; his hair is dirty and uncombed, and he has a penchant for liquor in mini-bar bottles --- watch him grow before your eyes. His editor is played by Bill Nighy; he may look like Peter O'Toole's son, but he's as tough as Ben Bradlee. Cal's closest colleague is young and female. In an American production, she'd be a hottie; here, she's from Scotland, and her accent is sufficiently thick that you may want to activate the subtitles.

And the dialogue! When the cops show up in the newsroom, the editor is wonderfully arch: "If you want to talk to busy people, it is best to make an appointment. Otherwise, you risk disappointment." Later, when reporters ask if they can run the story, he deadpans: "How much paper do you think you'll need?"

After the first episode, the reviewer for The Guardian wrote that "State of Play" is "bloody magic... If you can count the best dramas of recent years on the fingers of both hands, it's time to grow a new finger."

Typical British understatement.

This one's worth owning, if only to loan it to one grateful friend at a time. ■

"THE CONFORMIST"

What kind of man gets himself in such a
pickle that --- on his honeymoon --- he's
given a gun and asked to kill a professor
he's always admired?

That's the question presented at the beginning of
"The Conformist," as Marcello Clerici (Jean-Louis
Trintignant) sits in a Paris hotel room, waiting for
the call that will tell him it's time to kill the professor. If you love movies, the answer --- told in a series of flashbacks, and, on occasion, flashbacks
within flashbacks --- will make for one of the most
rewarding cinematic experiences of your life.

Let's get the praise out of the way right off. Bernardo Bertolucci --- known to most
moviegoers for his Oscar-winning "The Last Emperor" and his down-and-dirty "Last
Tango in Paris" --- made "The Conformist" at 29. It is a young man's film, drenched
in ambition. It is also Bertolucci's greatest film. Indeed, it is one of the ten greatest
films I've ever seen.

My reasons?

First, "The Conformist" is beautiful in the extreme. The cinematographer was the
great Vittorio Storaro, and his color palette is so exquisite that Francis Ford Cop-
pola watched this film over and over before making "The Godfather" --- and then
hired Storaro to shoot "Apocalypse Now." The production designer was Ferdinando
Scarfiotti, whose credits include "Death in Venice" and "Scarface." And Georges
Delerue, who did the scores for "Jules and Jim" and "Platoon," composed the music.

Then there is the acting. Trintignant, one of the most familiar faces in French cinema, gives the performance of his life. But I mostly want to praise Dominique Sanda,
then just 22 years old and making only her third movie. She plays the professor's
wife, and she unfailingly strikes a remarkable balance --- on one hand, she's the
loyal spouse, on another, she's a bi-sexual flirt, and on yet a third, she's the only
character in the story who senses the tragedy that lies ahead.

And, finally, there is the story, adapted from a novel by Alberto Moravia, one of Italy's most seductive writers. Sex is almost a character for Moravia, and it certainly is
here --- as the title suggests, Clerici's greatest desire is to be normal, to be one of the

faceless masses, to conform.

That's not so easily done in Italy in 1936. Mussolini has brought down the Fascist boot; progressives have fled the country. So Clerici takes a rich, vapid wife. He makes his accommodation with the government. And with that --- he thinks --- he's safe.

But there are no hiding places in life --- and certainly not in a dictatorship of madmen. And then there is the question of the past: How do you acquire a "normal" life if you never had one before? As we flash back, we see that Clerici's privileged childhood was anything but normal. His mother awoke at noon, looking for her first shot of the day. He was raised by nannies. And then there was the encounter with the chauffeur...

What Bertolucci is exploring here is the equation of politics with sex. In a film financed by an American studio, that equation would be explicit and vulgar. Here, every connection is made through imagery and suggestion. Your jaw will drop at scene after scene, but you'll be on the edge of your seat during one in particular --- an evening at a Parisian dance hall when Sanda dances with Professor's wife. It's a breathtaking seduction, hotter in some ways than sex itself.

Why does Clerici freeze when he's given a gun? Can he kill the professor? What happens to Sanda? And, jumping ahead, what does the Fascist defeat mean for Clerici? Bertolucci's screenplay is brilliant on these key questions; you are always leaning in, thinking it through, putting the puzzle together. And, of course, you are invited to imagine --- as we always do in great films --- how would I handle this? What would I do if I were Clerici? ∎

"Winter's Bone"

Jennifer Lawrence was just 21 when she played the needy, mouthy policeman's widow in "Silver Linings Playbook." This was her first Best Actress Academy Award, but it wasn't her first Oscar nomination. At 20, she was nominated for "Winter's Bone," her first starring role. That nomination made her the second-youngest actress ever nominated for the Academy Award for Best Actress. (At 21, she was also Katniss Everdeen in "The Hunger Games.")

In an ensemble cast of "Playbook," hers was the performance that held the movie together. This is equally true of her work in "Winter's Bone"--- she was so completely Ree Dolly that critics couldn't imagine another actress in the role. But few moviegoers have seen that breakthrough performance; made for $2 million, "Winter's Bone" grossed less than $7 million in American theaters.

We find ourselves among the rural poor in the bleak Ozarks of Missouri: cramped trailers, plastic stretched over the windows in winter, not a Volvo in sight. And the Dollys are among the most wretched.

Ree's father, Jessup Dolly, was busted a while back for cooking methamphetamine. To make bond, he put up his family's house and 300 acres of virgin timber. Now his court date is a week away --- and he's nowhere to be found. The local lawman warns Ree that the Dollys are in danger of losing their home.

Ree's mother has suffered a breakdown and is of no help, either in caring for her children or finding her husband. Which makes 17-year-old Ree responsible for her young sister and brother --- and for tracking her father down.

Ree's quest is a walk on a knife edge; she can't turn in her father, she can only ask for help in finding him so she can talk to him. And the only people who can help her? His relatives. Some of them make the most addictive drug on the planet. All of them don't understand why she can't remember she's a Dolly --- "bred and buttered," as she says --- and just stop. As they say, "Talking just causes witnesses."

Much of the cast is local and non-professional --- and, no offense, but they look like people who might make crank, who could scare the shit out of you at traffic lights with a sidelong glance, who would quiet you once with "I already told you to shut up with my mouth" and let their hands do the talking after that.

"Winter's Bone" won the Grand Jury Prize for Dramatic Films and the Waldo Salt Screenwriting Award at Sundance. In 2011, it received four Academy award nominations: Best Picture, Best Adapted Screenplay, Best Supporting Actor and Best Actress. Lawrence was up against Natalie Portman ("Black Swan"), Nicole Kidman ("Rabbit Hole"), Annette Bening ("The Kids Are Alright") and Michelle Williams ("Blue Valentine"). Portman won. Fine. But she too has given better performances.

"Winter's Bone" is both painful to watch and impossible to turn away from. The scene with the squirrel. Ree's desperate attempt to convince an Army recruiter --- who's played by an Army recruiter --- to let her enlist for five years so she can collect the government's $40,000 bonus. And a climax so remarkable, so distant from anything you know as reality, that you'll never forget it. ∎

"Without Limits"

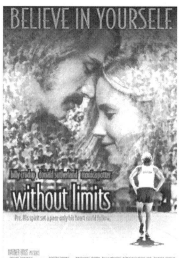

There are artists who paint by the rules. We call their work "decorative" and forget their names fast.

Then there are artists who break the rules and make something new, forcing us to see the world fresh.

They're the immortals.

Steve Prefontaine said, "Some people create with words or with music or with a brush and paints. I like to make something beautiful when I run. I like to make people stop and say, 'I've never seen anyone run like that before.' It's more than just a race, it's a style. It's doing something better than anyone else. It's being creative."

Prefontaine didn't have a low opinion of himself. But he got it right; he was an artist. He took the formula of long-distance running --- hang back, let the front-runner burn himself out, then kick at the end --- and spat on it. Pacing yourself, he believed, was for wimps. His style was to sprint. From start to finish. Go out fast, take the lead, keep the lead --- at any cost.

No one had ever run this way. But Steve Prefontaine, painting in time and space, did the impossible, proving that it wasn't impossible at all. He revolutionized long-distance running. Became a hero, a role model, a legend.

Was he driven? Of course. He grew up in a hard place --- the logging town of Coos Bay, Oregon --- and there weren't a lot of ways out. He started running as a kid, saw he was good at it, and amped up his effort. It's a simple story: the guy who wins because he can't afford to lose. "Somebody may beat me," he said, "but they are going to have to bleed to do it."

He wanted desperately to go to the University of Oregon at Eugene, but Bill Bowerman --- the legendary coach and, later, co-founder of Nike --- didn't believe in recruiting. But he did send his assistant, Bill Dellinger, to watch Prefontaine at the Oregon State high school cross-country meet. "I had my binoculars and I was probably a good half-mile, 700 yards away, from the start," Dellinger has recalled, "and I saw this guy as they were called to the line and got to the set position. I saw the look in his eyes, even from a half-mile distance, and the intensity in his face as the gun went off, and I thought that's gotta be Pre."

Prefontaine did go to Eugene. He bonded with Bowerman, and he won and won and won ---until the Munich Olympics in 1972. He returned to Oregon, committed to take a medal in 1976. And then, in 1975, he died in a car crash. He was 25.

An athlete dying young is an instant legend. Pre was made for the part. He had long dirty-blond hair, a moustache, fierce eyes --- he was the James Dean of running. Attitude? His mouth was always too candid by half. Charisma? His fans called themselves "Pre's People," and they came out every time he ran at Eugene's Hayward Field, screaming "Pre! Pre! Pre!" He loved them right back: "How can you lose with 12,000 people behind you?" And, in fact, he never lost a race over a mile on that track.

Prefontaine was the natural subject for a film. Twenty years after his death, there were two. The one you want to see is "Without Limits," co-written and directed by Robert Towne, whose writing credits include "Chinatown." Conrad Hall, who won an Oscar for "Butch Cassidy," was the cinematographer. Billy Crudup played Pre. Donald Sutherland was Bill Bowerman.

A distinguished team, but the film made little money and disappeared. That's tragic, because "Without Limits" is not just inspiring --- hell, most sports movies built around a dead guy are inspiring --- it's thrilling. In Hollywood, they talk about the "arc" of film stories. This has the arc of classic movies. A little guy digs deep, finds a big guy inside --- just without the car races and jet fighters that make so many of those films corny.

The races are blood-pounding; that's a given. But it's what's between them that makes the movie --- Pre was as funny as he was profane. There's a great scene, for example, when Bowerman comes to visit Pre in Coos Bay. He's brought along two of his star runners as advertisements for his program at Eugene. Pre turns to them: "How about an easy 10?" And off they go, into the woods. Cut to: their return. Pre is fresh, the college boys are barely able to breathe.

If you have a kid who needs to get his/her ass off the couch, here's your Saturday night viewing. If you're feeling sluggish, ditto. But be warned: "Without Limits" is as seductive as Prefontaine himself --- and as motivating. It can make the lame throw off their crutches, the faint of heart leap for the sky. See it, and believe. ■

Made in the USA
Lexington, KY
22 January 2014